Media Law in Italy

Media Law in Italy

Roberto Mastroianni
Amedeo Arena

This book was originally published as a monograph in the International Encyclopaedia of Laws/Media Law.

Founding Editor: Roger Blanpain
General Editor: Frank Hendrickx
Volume Editors: Peggy Valcke & Eva Lievens

Wolters Kluwer

Published by:
Kluwer Law International B.V.
PO Box 316
2400 AH Alphen aan den Rijn
The Netherlands
E-mail: lrs-sales@wolterskluwer.com
Website: www.wolterskluwer.com/en/solutions/kluwerlawinternational

Sold and distributed by:
Wolters Kluwer Legal & Regulatory U.S.
920 Links Avenue
Landisville, PA 17538
United States of America
E-mail: customer.service@wolterskluwer.com

ISBN 978-94-035-0947-1

e-Book: ISBN 978-94-035-0797-2
web-PDF: ISBN 978-94-035-0807-8

The Authors

Roberto Mastroianni is since 2000 a Full Professor of European Union (EU) Law at the University 'Federico II' in Naples, Italy and since September 2019, Judge of the Court of Justice of the EU (General Court). He also teaches at the University of Luxembourg, LLM Programs. Before his appointment at the CJEU as an attorney specializing in EU law and media law, he argued several cases before the same Court, the ECHR and national Courts. He graduated in Law from the University of Florence, Italy (1987), and holds a PhD in European Law from the University of Bologna (1991), as well as an LLM from the Penn State/Dickinson School of Law in Carlisle (PA), USA (1992). He specialized in International Copyright Law and European Media Law at the Universities of Geneva, Amsterdam and New York (NYLS). Former Researcher of International Law at the University of Florence (1992–1997), he served as *Referendaire* at the European Court of Justice (ECJ), in the Cabinets of Advocate General Giuseppe Tesauro and Antonio Saggio (1997–2000). He is the author of two handbooks on EU institutional and procedural law, several monographs and articles in European Law, Media Law and International Law, and has contributed to the publications of the Council of Europe's European Audiovisual Observatory and to research projects of the European institutions in the area of media law.

Amedeo Arena is a Full Professor of EU Law at the University of Naples Federico II. He graduated in Law from the University of Rome, completed a PhD in International Law from the University of Naples Federico II, and holds LLM degrees from King's College London and New York University, where he was also a Fulbright Fellow. He was Visiting Fellow at the Institute of Information Law at the University of Amsterdam and at the Institute of European and Comparative Law at Oxford University. His publications have been cited, *inter alia*, by the EU Court of Justice, the EU Agency for Fundamental Rights, the Portuguese Constitutional Court, and the Court of Appeal of England and Wales. A regular contributor to the publications of the Council of Europe's European Audiovisual Observatory, he served as an expert on Italian Media Law in studies conducted on behalf of the EU Institutions and the European Broadcasting Union.

Prof. Mastroianni has written §§ 1 and 2 of the General Introduction, Part I, Part II, Chapter 4 of Part III, and Part IV. Prof. Arena has written §3 of the General Introduction, Part III (except for Chapter 4), and Part V. The Authors would like to thank Dr Claudia Massa (University of Naples Federico II) and Dr Giovanna De Sanctis (AGCom) for their invaluable help in updating this monograph.

Table of Contents

List of Abbreviations

AGCom	*Autorità per le Garanzie nelle Comunicazioni*, the Italian Communications Authority
AVMS	Audiovisual Media Services
AVMSD	Audiovisual Media Services Directive (Directive 2010/13/EU as amended by Directive (EU) 2018/1808)
BEREC	Body of European Regulators for Electronic Communications
CIN	Commission for Infrastructures and Networks
CLAVMS	Consolidated Law on Audiovisual and Media Services (Legislative Decree no. 208/2021)
CLARMS	Consolidated Law on Audiovisual and Radio Media Services
CORECOM	*Comitati regionali per le comunicazioni*
CSP	Commission for Services and Products
DGs	Directorates-General
DTT	Digital Terrestrial Television
DGERP	Directorate-General for Electronic communications, Radio broadcasting, and Postal services, within the Ministry of Economic Development (*Direzione generale per i servizi di comunicazione elettronica, di radiodiffusione e postali, presso il Ministero dello sviluppo economico*)
ECHR	European Convention on Human Rights
ECJ	European Court of Justice
ECtHR	European Court of Human Rights
ECTT	European Convention on Transfrontier Television
EU	European Union
FIFA	Fédération Internationale de Football Association
GDPR	General Data Protection Regulation (Regulation EU 2016/679)
GDEI	Gruppo Editoriale S.p.A.
HD	High-Definition
ICS	Integrated Communications System
IPTV	Internet Protocol Television

List of Abbreviations

ISP	Internet Service Provider
ITU	International Telecommunications Union
NAPF	National Plan for the Assignment of Frequencies to the Digital Terrestrial Television Service
NCU	National Council of Users or *Consiglio nazionale degli utenti*
NGO	Non-governmental Organization
OJEU	Official Journal of the European Union
OJIR	Official Journal of the Italian Republic
PDPA	Personal Data Protection Authority (Garante per la Protezione dei Dati Personali)
PDPC	Personal Data Protection Code (Legislative Decree no. 196/2003, as subsequently amended)
PSC	Parliamentary Supervision Committee
PSM	Public Service Media
RAI	RAI-Radiotelevisione Italiana S.p.A.
RCO	Registry of Communications Operators
RTI	Reti Televisive Italiane S.p.A.
TEU	Treaty on European Union
TFEU	Treaty on the Functioning of the European Union
TV	Television
TVWFD	Television without Frontiers Directive (Directive 89/552/EEC, as amended by Directive 97/36/EC)
UEFA	Union of European Football Associations

General Introduction

§1. General Background of the Country

I. Political and Legal System of the Country

A. Introduction

1. Italy is a unitary State, established as a constitutional monarchy in 1861 and transformed into a Parliamentary Republic on 2 June 1946, following the outcome of a referendum on the form of the Italian State. Between 1922 and 1943, Italy witnessed an authoritarian shift, as power was seized by the National Fascist Party, which significantly constrained the rights and freedoms enshrined in the Kingdom of Italy's constitution, the Albertine Statute of 1848.

Currently, Italy has a written democratic Constitution, resulting from the work of a Constituent Assembly formed by elected representatives of all the forces that contributed to the defeat of Nazi and Fascist forces on 25 April 1945. The Constitution entered into force on 1 January 1948 and has been amended several times since then. Most notably, Constitutional Law no. 3 of 2001 amended Chapter V of the Constitution, granting Regions additional powers, *inter alia*, in information matters and expressly stating that national legislation must comply with international and European Union (EU) Law. On 8 February 2022, the Italian parliament passed the latest amendment, which enshrines the protection of the environment, biodiversity and ecosystems, interests of future generations, and animal life in the Constitution.

B. Legislative, Executive, and Judicial Branch

2. One of the founding principles of the Italian Republic is the separation of powers. The legislative power rests with the Parliament, which can delegate it to the Government subject to specific limits and procedures set out in the Constitution. The Parliament is perfectly bicameral: its two houses, the Chamber of Deputies and the Senate of the Republic have the same powers and must pass the same bill before it can be promulgated by the President of the Republic and published in the Official Journal of the Italian Republic (OJIR).

3. The executive power is entrusted to the Government, which consists of the Council of Ministers, in turn consisting of the President of the Council of Ministers (i.e., Italy's Prime Minister) and the Ministers, as well as vice-Ministers, undersecretaries of State, etc. The President of the Italian Republic appoints the President of the Council of Ministers and, on his or her proposal, the Ministers. The Government must obtain a vote of confidence by both houses of Parliament to take up office. The President of the Council of Ministers cannot request the dissolution of the Parliament or dismiss the Ministers (those are exclusive prerogatives of the President of the Republic) and must receive a vote of approval from the Council of Ministers to exercise some of its powers.

4. The judicial power is prevalently vested in professional judges, appointed for life following selection through a public competition. Ordinary members of the judiciary deal with most legal matters (ranging from civil to criminal law), except for specific categories of cases such as administrative matters, which are entrusted to administrative courts, and constitutional matters, which are entrusted exclusively to the Constitutional Court. The highest-ranking ordinary court is the Court of Cassation; the Council of State is the highest administrative court.

As Italy is a Civil Law system, precedent is not binding, with the exception of rulings by the Constitutional Court striking down unconstitutional laws. However, judgments delivered by the Court of Cassation and the Council of State are generally regarded as persuasive sources of guidance by lower courts.

C. The Vertical Division of Powers Between the State and the Regions

5. Italy is subdivided into twenty regions, five of which (Sicily, Sardinia, Aosta Valley, Trentino-Alto Adige/Südtirol and Friuli-Venezia Giulia) have a special Statute, conferring them additional powers over local matters.

6. Although the Italian Republic is, according to Article 5 of the Constitution, 'one and indivisible', it nonetheless 'recognizes and promotes local autonomy'.

The legislative power is exercised by the State and the Regions in keeping with the Constitution, as well as with EU and international law. The Constitution sets out an exhaustive list of matters over which the State has exclusive competence as well as a list of areas over which the State and the Regions have a shared competence. Matters not included in those lists are attributed to the Regions.

II. Geography and Population

7. Italy has a total area of 301,230 square kilometres and comprises the boot-shaped Italian Peninsula and a number of islands, the two largest being Sicily and Sardinia. Italy borders with France, Austria, Slovenia and Switzerland, as well as the two independent enclaves of San Marino and Vatican City.

8. Italy has a population of approximately 60 million, the third-largest in the EU (after Germany and France) and the twenty-fifth-largest worldwide.[1] The population density, at over 200 persons per square kilometre, is the fifth highest in the EU (after the Netherlands, Belgium, Luxembourg, and Germany). The highest density is in Northern Italy, which comprises almost half of the total population. Italy's most populated cities are Rome (2.8 million), Milan (1.3 million), Naples (0.97 million), and Turin (0.89 million).

III. Social and Cultural Values

9. Italy's official language is Italian, spoken by about 55 million in Italy and 6.7 million outside of the country.[2] Between 120 and 150 million people worldwide use Italian as a second or cultural language.[3]

As per Article 6 of the Constitution, Italy protects linguistic minorities. Several ethnic groups are legally recognized,[4] and a number of minority languages have co-official status, such as French (co-official in Aosta Valley), German (co-official in Trentino-Alto Adige), Ladin (spoken in certain parts of Trentino-Alto Adige and Veneto), and Slovene (officially recognized in the provinces of Trieste, Gorizia, and Udine).[5]

Roman Catholicism is by far the largest religion in the country, practised by 43.2 million Italians. Religious minorities among Italian citizens are: Muslims (493 thousand), Orthodox Christians (386 thousand), Protestant Christians (383 thousand), Jehovah's Witnesses (426 thousand), Buddhists (215 thousand), and others (84 thousand). Atheists and agnostics amount to 8.8 million.

§2. The Media Landscape

I. Overview of Media Markets and Main Actors

A. *Audio Visual Media Services (AVMS)*

10. The AVMS sector has undergone profound changes affecting production processes, business models, and consumption models.

---

1. ISTAT, Bilancio Demografico Anno 2020 (provisional data) available at: https://demo.istat.it/.
2. Ethnologue report for language code: ita (Italy), R. Gordon Jr (ed.), *Ethnologue: Languages of the World* (15th ed., SIL International, 2005). Online version, available at: www.ethnologue.com/show_language.asp?code=ita.
3. Italian Language: Geographic Distribution Discovery Media, available at: www.servinghistory.com/topics/Italian_language::sub::Geographic_Distribution.
4. *See* Constitutional Law 26 Feb. 1948, no. 4 (Special Statute for Aosta Valley); Constitutional Law 26 Feb. 1948, no. 5 (Special Statute for Trentino-Alto Adige); Constitutional Law 31 Jan. 1963, no. 1 (Special Statute for Friuli-Venezia Giulia).
5. *See* Art. 2 of Law 15 Dec. 1999, no. 482 laying down provisions for the protection of historic linguistic minorities (stating that the Italian Republic safeguards the language and culture of Albanian, Catalan, German, Greek, Slovenian, and Croatian communities, as well as of communities speaking French, Franco-Provençal, Friulian, Ladin, Occitan, and Sardinian).

11. Relative to the past, an increasing convergence is taking place in the ways in which users can enjoy audiovisual content. In this context, traditional broadcasters find themselves in competition with multiple operators, even outside the broadcasting sector, on multiple platforms and via multiple devices. Moreover, broadcasters often have on-demand platforms of their own.

12. Therefore, at the moment, the distinction between free-to-air Television (TV) (i.e., television broadcasters whose programmes can be viewed through a signal that can be enjoyed for free and is not encoded) and Pay-TV (i.e., television broadcasters whose programmes can only be viewed by purchasing or renting a specific decoder). based on the so-called product market appears obsolete, precisely in relation to the changes in the market itself. However, the data reported by the Italian Communications Regulation Authority shows that the largest share of the total economic resources (58.3%) is still attributable to the free audiovisual services market, which, despite the contraction of 7.2%, reached a value of EUR 4.4 billion in 2020. The reduction of the revenues of this market is mainly due to the negative dynamics of the advertising revenues, which show a trend in line with the macroeconomic evolution.

AVMS – Total Revenues for Free-to-Air TV (Million Euros)

	2015	2016	2017	2018	2019	2020	2021
Advertising	2.906	3.053	3.024	3.038	2.911	2.635	2.942
Canone	1.541	1.797	1.675	1.655	1.693	1.631	1.715
Subsidies/ Contracts	89	83	92	117	117	175	151
Total	**4.536**	**4.933**	**4.792**	**4.810**	**4.721**	**4.442**	**4.809**

Source: AGCom Annual Report 2022.

Free-to-Air TV (2020)

	Total	*Public Service Media Operator*	*Other Broadcasters*
Public Funds	40.7	93.9	6.1
Advertising	59.3	20.2	79.8

Source: AGCom Annual report 2021.

13. As regards Pay-TV, two trends have recently emerged: the first is the decrease in sports events due to the anti-pandemic regulations, which determined an 8.5% drop in subscriptions on Digital Terrestrial Television (DTT) and satellite television; the second is the huge growth in the use of films and entertainment due to the forced stay at home.

AVMS – Total Revenues for Pay-TV (Million Euros)							
	2015	2016	2017	2018	2019	2020	2021
Pay-TV offers	2.951	3.048	3.113	3.231	3.052	3.003	2.941
Advertising	342	337	320	302	244	168	141

Source: AGCom Annual Report 2022.

Pay-TV (%)		
	2019	2020
Pay-TV offers	92.6	94.7
Advertising	7.4	5.3

Source: AGCom Annual Report 2021.

Pay-TV offers (2020, %)			
	2019	2020	Change %2019/2020
DTT and Satellite TV pay content	2.546	2.330	–8.5
Paid web offers	473	674	42.5
Total	**3.019**	**3.003**	**–2.3**

Source: AGCom Annual report 2021.

14. For about a decade, the AVMS sector in Italy has shown a high degree of technological and market dynamism (with the entry of new national and international operators). Nonetheless, the traditional structure of the AVMS sector is still in place, with the three main incumbents (Sky/Comcast, Rai, Fininvest/Mediaset) having the largest market shares (almost 80% of the total resources), although their weight is decreasing compared to the past.

15. The remaining players are mostly the new Pay-TV operators (online platforms). They are acquiring the most attractive content for viewers. This trend has been reinforced also in the sports market with the recent acquisition of the sports rights of the *Serie A* football championship for the three-year period 2021–2024 by Dazn and with the assignment of the television rights of the Champions League to Amazon.

16. With regard to the audience, in relation to free-to-air and Pay-TV, there has been an increase in the audience of operators that have entered the market more recently and whose editorial offer is mainly thematic or semi-generalist. In contrast, the audience shares of traditional operators have decreased, although those operators still retain market leadership. Rai, in 2019, although witnessing a drop in its audience share, continues to be the largest operator (with over 3.5 million unique viewers per day), followed by Mediaset, which reaches shares that are largely higher than any other private operator in the sector with higher shares than any other private operator in the sector. Comcast/Sky Italia shows a slight increase, while Cairo shows a slight decrease in its audience; finally, Discovery and Viacom's channels are gaining around.

	Annual Average Day Audience Share (%)						
	2015	**2016**	**2017**	**2018**	**2019**	**2020**	**2021**
Rai	37.2	36.7	36.5	36.3	35.7	35.2	36,0
Fininvest/ Mediaset	32.4	31.6	31.3	31.2	31.6	32.1	31,9
Other operators	12.8	12.6	12.2	13.1	12.3	12.3	12,9
Discovery	6.3	6.7	6.9	6.7	7.4	7.7	7,4
Comcast/Sky Italia	6.7	7.9	8.4	7.0	7.2	6.5	6,2
Cairo Communication	3.6	3.7	3.4	4.2	4.2	3.8	3,7
Viacom	1.1	0.9	1.4	1.5	1.6	2.4	1,9
	100	**100**	**100**	**100**	**100**	**100**	**100**

Source: AGCom Annual Report 2022.

B. *Printed Press and Electronic Publishing*

17. The press market is characterized by a structural decline, caused by the reduction in the number of copies sold and advertising revenues. The structural crisis of the press market has not benefited from the increased demand for information due to the pandemic crisis. Despite the fact that newsstands were among the few commercial activities that could remain open and newspapers were among the primary sources of information, in the second trimester of 2020, only 17.6% of Italians chose to read newspapers. The downward trend in the daily reading of newspapers is, however, a common phenomenon in all European countries.

Newspapers, in particular, maintained their peculiar connotation as information-focused means of communication. Since 2012, however, there has been a steady decline in the number of newspapers printed and sold, along with a collapse in advertising revenues. While still representing the public's main source of information, in 2019, the number of copies sold on an average day fell below the critical 2-million threshold. There are several reasons for this development. First, the digitization processes have hit the daily press hardest, which started out as an analogue product and still has great difficulty in the process of transformation into a new way of accessing information. The fixed costs of producing the first copy continue to be high, while the costs of reproduction and distribution have fallen dramatically. Indeed, with the digitization of the information product, news has become a commodity that can be easily reproduced, distributed and consumed, sometimes free of charge. There is also a decrease in the time devoted to fact-checking, source reliability and quality control of the content, as well as an increase in the number of active supply-side operators. The active supply-side operators often do not fall within the perimeter of the classic publisher and their product provides users with the possibility of participating in the production and reproduction of information content. One of the most relevant aspects concerns the role of online platforms and their function as gatekeepers for access to information. They are an essential gateway for publishers to reach their readers and this affects the distribution strategies of each publisher for information content. In fact, the algorithms that govern the functioning of online platforms play a decisive role in determining how users use information, significantly directing the success or otherwise in terms of an audience of one news item – or even of a publisher – compared to another. In light of the above considerations, it is evident how the source of revenues from the sale of copies of printed and digital daily newspapers is going through a deep and lasting crisis, which inevitably reflects on the ability of the printed product to be valued also on the advertising side.

Revenues: value, incidence and changes in 2020 compared to 2019

	2019 (m €)	*2020* (m €)	*Incidence 2019 (%)*	*Incidence 2020 (%)*	Δ *2020–2019 (%)*
Revenue from the user	1.023	914	60.8	63.3	-10.6
Advertising	612	482	36.4	33.4	-21.2
Other revenues	47	47	2.8	3.3	0
Total	**1.682**	**1.444**			**-14.2**

Source: AGCom Annual report 2021.

Finally, as far as the main publishing groups are concerned, it should be noted that the GEDI group (GEDI Gruppo Editoriale S.p.A.) remains the leading operator with a market share of 17.6%, below the 20% concentration limit for daily press set out in Article 3 of Law no. 67/1987, followed by Cairo with a share of 16.2%. The other operators were all below 10%. It should also be noted that in 2021, the GEDI group reached an agreement for the sale of the business unit of the newspapers *Il Tirreno*, *La Gazzetta Di Modena*, *La Gazzetta Di Reggio* and *La Nuova Ferrara* to the company SAE S.r.l., whose effects will be evident during the current year.

II. Broadcasting Infrastructure

18. The broadcasting infrastructure situation in Italy is currently in a state of flux following the digital switchover, which has caused an *en bloc* audience transition from Analogue TV to DTT. Satellite TV accounts for 15.5% of the total audience. Internet Protocol Television (IPTV), instead, has still a very marginal role.

AVMS – Audience Share for Each Platform (%)		
	March 2012	March 2013
Analogue TV	11	0
DTT	71.9	84.4
Satellite TV	16.6	15.%
IPTV	0.2	0.1
Total	**100**	**100**

Source: AGCom Annual report 2011.

III. Technological and Economic Developments on the Media Markets

19. The AVMS sector in Italy has faced profound changes, especially after the conversion to the digital standard. Traditional broadcasters have tried to attract users throughout the day by offering multiplatform content. In fact, today, thanks to the interconnections between devices, it is possible to watch streaming programs on PCs, tablets and smartphones, live and on demand. The AVMS sector in Italy has faced profound changes following the conversion to digital. TV sets and decoders are now connected to the Internet and audiovisual content offered on traditional TV is also available online and on portable devices. The clearest examples are represented by Rai with the *Raiplay* platform and Mediaset with *Mediasetplay.*

20. The digital terrestrial transmission has changed in recent years. In particular, there has been a shift for DTT channels, which on 21 December 2022 abandoned the MPEG-2 standard to embrace MPEG-4 (previously used only by HD channels). In particular, the reception of TV programmes is now only possible with new generation TV sets or decoders, i.e., those equipped with the new transmission and encoding standards (DVBT-2/HEVC). A TV bonus for the replacement of TV sets has been envisaged.

21. The Ministry of Economic Development has set up the 'TV 4.0' coordination table. Representatives of the relevant institutions, television operators and the relevant trade associations participate in the work of the Table. The Table's objective is to harmonize and coordinate the activities for the release of the 700 MHz band and elaborate tools to favour the digital transformation of the TV sector.

§3. SOURCES OF MEDIA LAW

I. International and EU Law Relevant to Media Matters

A. *The Status of International and EU Law in the Italian Legal Order*

22. Article 117, paragraph 1, of the Constitution, provides that the exercise of legislative power by both the State and the Regions must comply with EU and international obligations.

As far as customary international law is concerned, Article 10, paragraph 1, of the Constitution provides that the Italian legal order conforms to generally recognized principles of international law.

Moreover, under Article 11 of the Constitution, Italy agrees to limitations of sovereignty required by a legal order seeking to ensure peace and justice between nations. The Constitutional Court ruled that Article 11 of the Constitution constitutes the basis for the transfer of sovereignty to the EU inherent in the European integration process.[6]

23. In view of the status that international law and EU law enjoy in the Italian legal order, national legislation incompatible with an international or an EU provision is unconstitutional. Should such an antinomy be detected in the course of proceedings before a Court, the latter must stay proceedings and refer the matter to the Constitutional Court, which will strike down the relevant national provision.[7] Instead, if the conflict involves a national provision and an EU provision having direct effect, courts must immediately set aside the former provision and apply the latter, without having recourse to the referral mechanism to the Constitutional Court outlined above.[8]

Since 2017, however, the Constitutional Court has championed a centralization of judicial review of Italian legislation at variance with fundamental rights as protected both by the Italian Constitution and the EU Charter of Fundamental Rights.[9] Moreover, the Constitutional Court has consistently held that the Italian legal order does not open up unconditionally to EU law. Accordingly, the Court reserved the right to review the compatibility of EU law with the basic principles of the Italian legal order and the inviolable right of individuals (the so-called *controlimiti* doctrine).[10] So far the Constitutional Court has never exercised the rights flowing from this doctrine, although it came close to doing so in the context of the so-called *Taricco* saga.[11]

---

6. *See* Constitutional Court, Judgment no. 183/73 and no. 232/75.
7. Constitutional Court, Judgment nos 348/2007, 349/2007, 311/2009, and 227/2010.
8. Constitutional Court, Judgment nos 113/1985, 168/1991, 232/1989, 389/1989, and 284/2007.
9. *See* Constitutional Court, Judgment nos 269/2017, 117/2019, 182/2021.
10. *See* Constitutional Court, Judgment no. 168/91. *See also* Constitutional Court, Judgment nos 183/73, 232/75, and 232/89.
11. Constitutional Court, order no. 24/2017 and judgment no. 115/18.

B. International Agreements

24. There are a number of international agreements relevant to the regulation of media in Italy.[12] Among them, regard must be had, first and foremost, to the International Covenant on Civil and Political Rights, adopted by the United Nations General Assembly on 16 December 1966 and ratified by Italy on 15 September 1978.[13]

Article 19 of the said Covenant enshrines the principle of freedom of expression. That provision allows for restrictions provided by law and necessary for respect of the rights or reputation of others and for the protection of national security, public order, public health, and public morals.

In its instrument of ratification, Italy included the following reservation to that provision:

The provisions of Article 19, paragraph 3, are interpreted as being compatible with the existing licensing system for national radio and television and with the restrictions laid down by law for local radio and television companies and for stations relaying foreign programmes.[14]

25. Italy joined the International Telecommunications Union (ITU) on 1 January 1966. The Radio Regulations, which are updated by ITU every four years, are of particular relevance to the management of the broadcasting spectrum. In Italy, those Regulations are taken into account by the Ministry of Economic Development when, every five years, it draws up the national spectrum distribution plan.

C. The European Convention of Human Rights and the Convention on Transfrontier Television

26. Turning to regional agreements, Italy – a founding member of the Council of Europe – ratified both the Convention for the Protection of Human Rights and Fundamental Freedoms, signed in Rome on 4 November 1950 (hereafter: the ECHR),[15] and the European Convention on Transfrontier Television (ECTT), signed in Strasbourg on 5 May 1989.[16]

In particular, Article 10 ECHR safeguards the freedom to hold opinions and to receive and impart information and ideas without interference by public authority and regardless of frontiers.

27. The principle enshrined in Article 10 ECHR has several corollaries, such as the freedom of reception and retransmission set out in Article 4 ECTT, whereby the

12. *See* generally G. Strozzi, 'La libertà dell'informazione nel diritto internazionale', *Nuove dimensioni dei diritti di libertà: scritti in onore di Paolo Barile* (Padua: Cedam, 1990): 669 et seq.
13. *See* Law 25 Oct. 1977, no. 881 (authorizing the President of the Republic to ratify the Covenant).
14. United Nations, Note by the Secretary General, 'Reservations, declarations, notifications and objections relating to the International Covenant on Civil and Political Rights and the Optional Protocols thereto' (24 Aug. 1994, document no. CCPR/C/2/Rev.4).
15. *See* Law 4 Aug. 1955, no. 848 (authorizing the President of the Republic to ratify the ECHR).
16. *See* Law 5 Oct. 1991, no. 327 (authorizing the President of the Republic to ratify the ECTT).

parties to the ECTT undertake to guarantee freedom of reception and not to restrict the retransmission on their territories of programme services complying with the ECTT provisions.

28. Another corollary of Article 10 ECHR is the right to pluralistic information, which calls for *ex ante* regulation to prevent the creation of dominant positions. The principle of media pluralism has been stressed by the ECHR in a number of rulings[17] and is reflected in Article 10*bis* ECTT as well as in several recommendations and resolutions adopted by the Committee of Ministers and the Parliamentary Assembly of the Council of Europe.[18]

29. Article 10 ECHR also postulates the editorial and institutional independence of Public Service Media (hereafter: PSM) operators, which must be allowed to operate independently of those holding economic and political power.[19] The Parliamentary Assembly of the Council of Europe adopted a Resolution dealing specifically with the criticalities in the governance of the Italian PSM operator as well as the lack of pluralism in the media sector.[20]

D. EU Law

30. EU law is relevant to the regulation of media in Italy in several respects. Article 11 of the Charter of Fundamental Rights of the EU expressly recognizes the freedom of expression and, in particular, the need to respect the freedom and pluralism of media. As per Article 6, paragraph 3, of the Treaty on European Union (hereinafter: 'TEU') fundamental rights, as guaranteed by the ECHR and the constitutional traditions common to the Member States, constitute general principles of EU Law.

---

17. *See*, for example, European Court of Human Rights, *Informationsverein Lentia v. Austria*, series A, no. 276, §32; *Jersild*, series A, no. 298, §23; *Centro Europa 7 Srl v. Italy*, application no. 38433/09 §129. *See* E. Kowarek, *Is Media Pluralism a Human Right? The European Court of Human Rights, the Council of Europe and the Issue of Media Pluralism*, Eur. Human Rights L. Rev. 395 et seq. (2009).
18. *See*, for example, Council of Europe, Recommendation no. R (99) 1 of the Committee of Ministers to Member States on Measures to Promote Media Pluralism; Recommendation no. R (2003) 9 of the Committee of Ministers on measures to promote the democratic and social contribution of digital broadcasting; Recommendation 1506 (2001) of the Parliamentary Assembly on freedom of expression and information in the media in Europe; Recommendation 1589 (2003) of the Parliamentary Assembly on freedom of expression in the media in Europe.
19. Council of Europe, Recommendation 1641 (2004) of the Parliamentary Assembly on Public Service Broadcasting. *See also* Recommendation no. R (96) 10 of the Committee of Ministers to Member States on the Guarantee of the Independence of Public Service Broadcasting; Recommendation 1878 (2009) of the Parliamentary Assembly on the Funding of public service broadcasting.
20. Council of Europe, Resolution 1387 (2004) Monopolisation of the electronic media and possible abuse of power in Italy.

31. In this connection, the European Commission called for joint action to prevent media concentration in its 1992 Green Paper.[21] In 2007, the Commission published a background paper entitled 'Media pluralism in the Member States of the European Union', putting forward a definition of the concept of 'media pluralism' and outlining the main features of the notion of 'media concentration', including at the cross-border level.[22] The Commission was also instrumental in setting up the Media Pluralism Monitor.[23] So far, the Commission has not submitted a legislative proposal aimed at limiting or preventing media concentration but has addressed those issues only indirectly, through the enforcement of the EU rules on antitrust and merger control.[24]

32. The European Parliament has repeatedly called for action to protect media pluralism. It has adopted a number of resolutions stressing the importance of media pluralism in the EU as a whole[25] and voicing concerns in relation to developments in individual Member States, including Italy.[26] A European citizens' initiative was launched in 2013 calling for EU legislation harmonizing national rules on media ownership and transparency and setting EU standards for the independence of media supervisory bodies in Member States, but it failed in collecting the required number of signatures.[27] A new proposal for a Regulation on media freedom and pluralism has been tabled by the European Commission in September 2022[28] and is currently at the attention of the European Parliament and Council for its final adoption.

---

21. European Commission, Pluralism and Media Concentration in the Internal Market: An Assessment of the Need for Community Action, COM (92) 480 Final (23 Dec. 1992).
22. European Commission, Staff Working Paper Media pluralism in the Member States of the European Union, SEC (2007) 32 (16 Jan. 2007).
23. *See* K. Bania and E. Brogi, Instruments to measure media and publicize concentration: the example of the Media Pluralism Monitor, in M. Cappello (ed.), Media ownership: Market realities and regulatory responses, IRIS Special 2016-2, European Audiovisual Observatory, Strasbourg, 2016, pp. 35–48.
24. *See* M. Cole and S. Hans, Guaranteeing media diversity at European level, in M. Cappello (ed.), Media ownership: Market realities and regulatory responses, IRIS Special 2016-2, European Audiovisual Observatory, Strasbourg, 2016, pp. 20–28.
25. European Parliament, Resolution of 25 Sep. 2008 on concentration and pluralism in the media in the EU (2007/2253(INI)).
26. European Parliament, Resolution on the risks of violation, in the EU and especially in Italy, of freedom of expression and information (2003/2237), para. 59 (regretting 'the repeated and documented instances of governmental interference, pressure and censorship in respect of the corporate structure and schedules of the RAI public television service'). *See also* R. Craufurd Smith, *Rethinking European Union Competence in the Field of Media Ownership: The Internal Market, Fundamental Rights and European Citizenship*, 29 Eur. L. Rev., 652 et seq. (2004); R. Mastroianni, *Freedom and pluralism of the media: a European value waiting to be discovered?* Media Laws, 3 (2021).
27. *See* https://europa.eu/citizens-initiative/initiatives/details/2013/000007_en. *See* R. Mastroianni, 'Promoting Information Pluralism Through EU Law: Regulation or Competition Law in the Audiovisual Sector?', in *EU Competition Law Between Public and Private Enforcement,* ed. B. Cortese (Kluwer Law International, 2014), 333 et seq.
28. Proposal for a Regulation of the European Parliament and of the Council establishing a common framework for media services in the internal market (European Media Freedom Act) and amending Directive 2010/13/EU, COM/2022/457 final.

33. Turning to EU free movement law, the European Court of Justice (ECJ) held in *Sacchi* that television broadcasting can be regarded as a service within the meaning of Article 56 of the Treaty on the Functioning of the European Union (TFEU).[29] In subsequent cases, the ECJ clarified that internal market provisions cover any form of electromagnetic transmission of information across frontiers, including terrestrial and direct satellite broadcasting, and cable transmission.[30]

34. Since the provision of AVMS is an economic activity, it falls within the scope of the TFEU provisions on competition and State aid.[31] In particular, the financing of public service broadcasting is the subject of Protocol no. 29 on the system of public broadcasting in the Member States,[32] as well as Communication by the European Commission.[33]

35. In addition to the negative integration resulting from the application of the fundamental freedoms set out in the TFEU, several aspects of media regulation have been harmonized by the EU legislature, thus preempting national law-making powers in those areas. While a comprehensive analysis of the growing body of EU legislation in this area is beyond the scope of this work, regard will be given to the most important directives and regulations adopted in two areas: audiovisual media services (AVMS) and electronic communications.

36. As to AVMS, Member States' rules on linear AVMS (i.e., television broadcasting) were first harmonized by the Television without Frontiers Directive (the TVWFD, i.e., Directive 89/552/EEC,[34] as amended by Directive 97/36/EC).[35] That Directive was then amended by Directive 2007/65/EC[36] and codified as Directive

29. *See*, in particular, ECJ, Case 155/73, *Sacchi*, [1974] ECR 409, para. 6; Case 52/79, *Debauve*, [1980] ECR 833, para. 8; Case C-260/89, *ERT*, [1991] ECR I-2925, paras 20–25; Case C-353/ 89, *Commission v. Netherlands (Mediawet II)*, [1991] ECR I-4069, para. 38; Case C-211/91, *Commission v. Belgium*, [1992] ECR I-6757, para. 5; and Case C-23/93, *TV10*, [1994] ECR. I-4795, paras 13 and 16.
30. *See* ECJ, Case 62/79, *Coditel I*, [1980] ECR 881; Case 352/85, *Bond van Adverteerders*, [1988] ECR 2085; Joined Cases C-544 and C-545/03, *Mobistar*, [2005] ECR I-7723.
31. *See*, in particular, ECJ, Case C-69/13, *Mediaset SpA*, [2014], not published in *ECR*.
32. *See* generally R. Mastroianni, 'Il Protocollo sul sistema di radiodiffusione pubblica', *Il Diritto dell'Unione Europea* (1998): 533 et seq.
33. Communication from the Commission on the application of State aid rules to public service broadcasting.
34. Directive 89/552/EEC of the Council of 3 Oct. 1989 on the coordination of certain provisions laid down by Law, Regulation or Administrative Action in Member States concerning the pursuit of television broadcasting activities.
35. Directive 97/36/EC of the European Parliament and of the Council of 30 Jun. 1997 amending Council Directive 89/552/EEC on the coordination of certain provisions laid down by law, regulation or administrative action in Member States concerning the pursuit of television broadcasting activities.
36. Directive 2007/65/EC of the European Parliament and of the Council of 11 Dec. 2007 amending Council Directive 89/552/EEC on the coordination of certain provisions laid down by law, regulation or administrative action in Member States concerning the pursuit of television broadcasting activities.

2010/13/EU,[37] known as the Audiovisual Media Services Directive (AVMSD) because it applied both to linear AVMS and non-linear AVMS (i.e., on-demand services). The AVSMD was recently amended by Directive 2018/1808,[38] which seeks to strengthen the country-of-origin principle,[39] to extend certain audiovisual rules to video-sharing platforms and social media services, to protect minors against harmful content,[40] also in relation to video-sharing, platforms,[41] etc.[42] The EU legislature has not yet codified the AVMSD as amended by Directive 2018/1808,[43] but the Publications office of the EU has prepared a consolidated version.[44]

37. Moreover, the EU legislature, in the context of the Strategy for the Digital Single Market, has introduced a specific liability regime for online content-sharing platforms under Directive 2019/790/EU.[45]

38. The existing EU rules on AVMS will be complemented also by the rules contained in the so-called Digital Services Act,[46] a regulation whose adoption is expected in 2023. This proposed regulation focuses on issues such as the liability of online intermediaries for third-party content, safety of online users or asymmetric due diligence obligations for different providers of information society services depending on the nature of the societal risks such services represent. In concrete terms, this proposed regulation contains a set of new EU-level harmonized obligations that will apply to all digital services that connect consumers to goods, services or contents, and provides for new procedures for faster removal of illegal contents

---

37. Directive 2010/13/EU of the European Parliament and of the Council of 10 Mar. 2010 on the coordination of certain provisions laid down by law, regulation or administrative action in Member States concerning the provision of AVMS (Audiovisual Media Services Directive).
38. Directive (EU) 2018/1808 of the European Parliament and of the Council of 14 Nov. 2018 amending Directive 2010/13/EU on the coordination of certain provisions laid down by law, regulation or administrative action in Member States concerning the provision of AVMS (Audiovisual Media Services Directive) in view of changing market realities.
39. *See* Roberto Mastroianni, 'Country of origin' e principio di territorialità, in *Rivista di diritto dei media*, 2019, issue 1, pp. 42–59; Mark Cole, The AVMSD Jurisdiction Criteria concerning Audiovisual Media Service Providers after the 2018 Reform, 2018, available at: https://emr-sb.de/wp-content/uploads/2018/12/EMR_MDC_AVMSD-jurisdiction-after-2018-reform_12-2018-1.pdf.
40. *See* Filippo Donati, La tutela dei minori nella direttiva 2018/1808, *in Rivista di diritto dei media*, 2019, issue 1, pp. 60–72.
41. *See* Lubos Kuklis, Media regulation at a distance: video-sharing platforms in Audiovisual Media Services Directive and the future of content regulation, in *Rivista di diritto dei media*, 2020, issue 2, pp. 95–110.
42. *See* the European Commission's webpage on the Revision of the AVMSD: https://digital-strategy.ec.europa.eu/en/policies/revision-avmsd.
43. The Institute of European Media Law (EMR) has prepared a synopsis highlighting the changes between Directive 2010/13 and Directive 2018/1808. It is available at: https://emr-sb.de/wp-content/uploads/2019/03/EMR-Synopsis-AVMSD_short_EN.pdf.
44. Available at: https://eur-lex.europa.eu/legal-content/EN/TXT/?uri=CELEX:02010L0013-20181218.
45. Directive (EU) 2019/790 of the European Parliament and of the Council of 17 Apr. 2019 on copyright and related rights in the Digital Single Market and amending Directives 96/9/EC and 2001/29/EC.
46. Proposal for a Regulation of the European Parliament and of the Council on a Single Market For Digital Services (Digital Services Act) and amending Directive 2000/31/EC, COM/2020/825 final.

and a comprehensive protection of the fundamental rights of online users. The proposed regulation will complement existing sector-specific legislation and will not affect the application of existing EU instruments regulating certain aspects of the provision of information society services, which apply as *lex specialis*. Thus, the obligations set out in the AVSM Directive on video-sharing platform providers as regards audiovisual content and audiovisual commercial communications will continue to apply. However, this regulation will apply to those providers to the extent that the AVSMD or other EU acts, such as the proposal for a Regulation on addressing the dissemination of terrorist content online, do not contain more specific provisions applicable to them.

39. An impact on digital media regulation will also occur with the entry into force of the so-called Digital Markets Act,[47] another proposed regulation whose entry into force is expected in 2023. This proposed regulation is intended to combat unfair practices implemented by the largest providers of digital core platform services (such as online search engines, social networking, video-sharing platform services, advertising services, etc.) – the so-called gatekeepers (e.g., Google, Apple, Meta, Amazon and Microsoft) – and to address the problem of the lack of contestability in digital markets, which creates inefficiencies in terms of higher prices, lower quality, less choice and less innovation, to the detriment of European consumers.

40. The Electronic Communications Directives include: the Framework Directive,[48] the Access Directive,[49] the Authorization Directive,[50] the Universal Service Directive,[51] and the e-Privacy Directive.[52] Those directives were amended in 2009 by the Better Regulation Directive[53] and Citizens' Rights Directive[54] and complemented by Regulation 1211/2009/EC establishing the Body of European Regulators for Electronic Communications (BEREC).[55]

47. Proposal for a Regulation of the European Parliament and of the Council on contestable and fair markets in the digital sector (Digital Markets Act), COM/2020/842 final.
48. Directive 2002/21/EC of the European Parliament and of the Council of 7 Mar. 2002 on a common regulatory framework for electronic communications networks and services.
49. Directive 2002/19/EC of the European Parliament and of the Council of 7 Mar. 2002 on access to, and interconnection of, electronic communications networks and associated facilities.
50. Directive 2002/20/EC of the European Parliament and of the Council of 7 Mar. 2002 on the authorization of electronic communications networks and services.
51. Directive 2002/22/EC of the European Parliament and of the Council of 7 Mar. 2002 on universal service and users' rights relating to electronic communications networks and services.
52. Directive 2002/58/EC of the European Parliament and of the Council of 12 Jul. 2002 concerning the processing of personal data and the protection of privacy in the electronic communications sector.
53. Directive 2009/140/EC of 25 Nov. 2009 amending Directives 2002/21/EC on a common regulatory framework for electronic communications networks and services, 2002/19/EC on access to, and interconnection of, electronic communications networks and services, and 2002/20/EC on the authorization of electronic communications networks and services.
54. Directive 2009/136/EC of the European Parliament and of the Council of 25 Nov. 2009 amending Directive 2002/22/EC on universal service and users' rights relating to electronic communications networks and services, Directive 2002/58/EC concerning the processing of personal data and the protection of privacy in the electronic communications sector and Regulation (EC) no. 2006/ 2004

41. A number of regulatory interventions took place in the electronic communications sector after 2009. That is the case of Regulation (EU) 2015/2120,[56] for roaming in Member States, which provided for the abolition of the surcharge on top of domestic retail prices. Moreover, in the context of the Digital Single Market Strategy, the EU legislature recently adopted Directive (EU) 2018/1972 of the European Parliament and of the Council of 11 December 2018, establishing the European Electronic Communications Code.[57]

II. Constitutional Principles

42. The cornerstone provisions of the Italian Constitution dealing with media matters are Article 15 and Article 21. Article 15 stipulates that 'the freedom and confidentiality of correspondence and of every form of communication' are inviolable. Article 21 states that all individuals have the right 'to express their thoughts by speech, in writing, and by all other means of communication'.

Article 21 of the Constitution will be analysed in further detail in Part I concerning the freedom of speech. This section will address the relationship between Article 21 and Article 15 as well as the constraints placed by Article 21 upon the legislature in regulating the media sector.

A. *The Relationship Between the Freedom of Correspondence and the Freedom of Expression*

43. The relationship between Article 21 and Article 15 of the Constitution has been a source of debate for several years. Early commentators considered the freedom of correspondence set out in Article 15 a subcategory of the freedom of expression laid down in Article 21.[58] The Constitutional Court, instead, took the view that Article 15 and Article 21 of the Constitution are structurally and functionally independent: the freedom of correspondence serves the purpose of guaranteeing the privacy of individuals in private communications, whereas the freedom of expression seeks to protect the free flow of information and the pluralism of opinions as important factors for the democratic development of society.[59]

---

on cooperation between national authorities responsible for the enforcement of consumer protection laws. *See* F. Bassan (ed.), *Diritto delle comunicazioni elettroniche* (Milan: Giuffré 2010).

55. Regulation (EC) No 1211/2009 of the European Parliament and of the Council of 25 Nov. 2009 establishing the BEREC and the Office.
56. Regulation (EU) 2015/2120 of the European Parliament and of the Council of 25 Nov. 2015 laying down measures concerning open internet access and amending Directive 2002/22/EC on universal service and users' rights relating to electronic communications networks and services and Regulation (EU) No 531/2012 on roaming on public mobile communications networks within the Union, pp. 1–18.
57. Directive (EU) 2018/1972 of the European Parliament and of the Council of 11 Dec. 2018 establishing the European Electronic Communications Code (Recast), pp. 36–214.
58. C. Esposito, *La libertà di manifestazione del pensiero nell'ordinamento giuridico italiano* (Milano: Giuffrè, 1958).
59. Constitutional Court, judgment no. 1030 of 1988; Constitutional Court, judgment no. 81 of 1993.

44. Some authors argued that technological convergence – that is, the process by which the same distribution medium (e.g., the radio spectrum) can be used to convey different services – blurred the distinction between the freedom of correspondence and the freedom of expression.[60]

Most commentators, however, took the view that the above distinction is still valid, even in the context of the so-called new media.[61] In particular, the two freedoms can be distinguished on the basis of the purpose for which a given medium is employed: if the aim is to communicate with one or more recipients, then Article 15 of the Constitution applies, whereas if the purpose is to inform an undetermined plurality of recipients, then Article 21 applies.[62]

B. The Principle of '*Riserva Di Legge*' and the Constraints Placed upon the Legislature in Media Matters

45. The freedom of expression is safeguarded by the principle of *riserva di legge*, that is, the constitutional requirement that information and communication matters be regulated by laws enacted by the Parliament (*leggi*) or acts enjoying the same status in the hierarchy of legal sources (i.e., decree-laws or legislative decrees).[63]

46. The principle of *riserva di legge* constrains the discretion of the legislature, in that it can only place restrictions upon constitutional freedom protected by a *riserva di legge* to pursue an equally ranking goal enshrined in the Constitution. As far as the freedom of expression is concerned, for instance, Article 21, paragraph 7, of the Constitution expressly recognizes public morality as a legitimate ground to place restrictions upon that freedom.[64]

47. The principle of *riserva di legge* also places a positive obligation upon the legislature to regulate the matter concerned, thus preempting the executive's regulatory power in that area. In this connection, a distinction must be drawn between relative and absolute *riserva di legge*. If a matter is subject to an absolute *riserva di legge,* that matter must be comprehensively and exclusively regulated by laws passed by the Parliament or by acts adopted by the Government having equivalent legal status. The executive can only adopt measures designed to implement those legislative acts. In contrast, if a given matter is covered by a relative *riserva di*

60. *See* P. Caretti, *I diritti fondamentali* (Torino: Giappichelli, 2005), 212 et seq.; P. Costanzo, 'Le nuove forme di comunicazione in rete: Internet, in Informazione e telecomunicazione', in *Trattato di diritto amministrativo*, ed. G. Santaniello, XXVIII (Padova: Cedam, 1999), 323 et seq.
61. *See* G. Gardini, *Le Regole dell'Informazione. Verso la Gigabit Society* (Turin: Giappichelli, 2021); A. Pace, M. Manetti, 'Art. 21: la libertà di manifestazione del proprio pensiero', in *Commentario della Costituzione*, eds G. Branca, A. Pizzorusso (Bologna: Zanichelli, 2006), 17 et seq.
62. *See* G. Gardini, *Le Regole dell'Informazione. Verso la Gigabit Society* (Turin: Giappichelli, 2021).
63. R. Zaccaria, 'Radiotelevisione', in *Trattato di diritto amministrativo*, ed. G. Santaniello, XV, II (Padova: Cedam, 1996), 39 et seq.; P. Caretti, A. Cardone, *Diritto dell'informazione e della comunicazione nell'era della convergenza,* (Bologna: il Mulino, 2019).
64. P. Caretti, A. Cardone, *Diritto dell'informazione e della comunicazione nell'era della convergenza* (Bologna: il Mulino, 2019).

legge, the legislature must only establish the guiding principles of the legal framework, whose detailed content is to be determined by the executive.

48. Some scholars suggested that the *riserva di legge* set out in Article 21 of the Constitution has a relative character, as in the case of Articles 41 and 42 of the Constitution (concerning, respectively, the freedom of enterprise and the right of property), two provisions that frequently come into play in broadcasting matters.[65] The Constitutional Court, however, in its Judgment no. 112/1993, clarified that the *riserva di legge* laid down in Article 21 of the Constitution is of an absolute type.[66]

49. The *riserva di legge* set forth in Article 21 of the Constitution, finally, constrains the margin of discretion enjoyed by authorities endowed with enforcement powers in that area (including AGCom, the Italian Communications Authority). Those authorities must act within the limits set out in primary legislation and can only pursue the goals set out therein.

III. Primary Legislation

A. Categories of Primary Legislation

50. The category of primary legislation includes laws enacted by the Parliament (*leggi*) and acts adopted by the Government having the same rank as laws in the hierarchy of legal sources, that is to say, Decree-Laws (*decreti legge*) and Legislative Decrees (*decreti legislativi*).

51. Laws, also known as 'Ordinary Laws' (*leggi ordinarie),* are numerically the most relevant category of primary legislation. The right of legislative initiative rests with the Government, each Member of the Italian Parliament, or 50,000 voters. Bills must be passed by both the Chamber of Deputies and the Senate of the Republic and promulgated by the President of the Republic. Except as otherwise provided, laws enter into force on the fifteenth day following their publication in the OJIR.

52. Legislative decrees are adopted by the Government on the basis of an enabling law (*legge delega*) adopted by the Parliament setting out the guidelines that the Government must follow in exercising its delegated legislative power as well as the temporal and material scope of that delegation.[67] Should the Government overstep the bounds of its delegated power, the relevant Legislative Decree is unconstitutional and can be struck down by the Constitutional Court.

53. Decree-laws can only be adopted by the Government in case of necessity and urgency and must be submitted to the Parliament for conversion into laws on

65. A. Pace, 'La radiotelevisione in Italia con particolare riferimento all'emittenza privata', in *Rivista Trimestrale di Diritto Pubblico* (1987): 644.
66. Constitutional Court, Judgment of 24–26 Mar. 1993, no. 112.
67. *See* Art. 76 of the Constitution.

the same day as their adoption. Decree-laws become ineffective retroactively if they are not converted into laws by the Parliament within sixty days of their publication in the OJIR.[68] The Constitutional Court, in its Judgment no. 360 of 1996, held that the Government cannot adopt subsequent decree-laws having the same content to elude that deadline.[69]

B. Notable Items of Primary Legislation in the Media Sector

54. In view of the *riserva di legge* set out in Article 21 of the Constitution, it is no wonder that Parliament legislation has played a major role in the regulation of the media sector. The Press Law,[70] the Journalist Profession Law,[71] as well as several laws on broadcasting matters (e.g., the Mammì Law,[72] the Maccanico Law[73] and the Gasparri Law),[74] were ordinary laws enacted by the Parliament. In particular, it was an ordinary law (the Maccanico Law) that established AGCom, the Italian Communications Authority.

55. In recent years, the Government has become a co-protagonist in regulating media matters. This is apparently at odds with the centrality of Parliament that the Constitutional Court advocated in this area.[75] As a matter of fact, the key items of media legislation currently in force are legislative decrees adopted by the Government: that is the case of Legislative Decree no. 259/2003 (‘Electronic Communications Code’),[76] Legislative Decree no. 207/2021[77] (transposing Directive 2018/1972 establishing the European Electronic Communications Code (Recast)), Legislative Decree no. 208/2021[78] transposing Directive 2018/1808 and repealing Legislative Decree no. 177/2005[79] (the ‘Consolidated Law on Audiovisual Media Services’, CLAVMS).

---

68. Articles 76 and 77 of the Constitution.
69. Constitutional Court, Judgment of 17 Oct. 1996, no. 360.
70. Law 8 Feb. 1948, no. 47, ‘Disposizioni sulla stampa’.
71. Law 3 Feb. 1963, no. 69, ‘Ordinamento della professione di giornalista’.
72. Law 6 Aug. 1990, no. 223, ‘Disciplina del sistema radiotelevisivo pubblico e privato’ (the ‘Mammì Law’).
73. Law 31 Jul. 1997, no. 249, ‘Istituzione dell’Autorita’ per le garanzie nelle comunicazioni e norme sui sistemi delle telecomunicazioni e radiotelevisivo’ (the ‘Maccanico Law’.
74. Law 3 May 2004, no. 112, ‘Norme di principio in materia di assetto del sistema radiotelevisivo e della RAI-Radiotelevisione italiana Spa, nonché delega al Governo per l’emanazione del testo unico della radiotelevisione’ (the ‘Gasparri Law’).
75. Constitutional Court, Judgment nos 225 and 226 of 1974.
76. Legislative Decree no. 259 of 1 Aug. 2003, ‘Codice delle Comunicazioni Elettroniche (“Electronic Communications Code” or ECC’). This decree was adopted to implement the 2002 and 2009 Directives on Electronic Communications. The Electronic Communications Code repealed and replaced most of the provisions of the Postal Code adopted in 1973 (Decree of the President of the Republic 29 Mar. 1973, no. 156).
77. Legislative Decree no. 207 of 8 Nov. 2021, ‘Attuazione della direttiva (UE) 2018/1972 del Parlamento europeo e del Consiglio, dell’11 dicembre 2018, che istituisce il Codice europeo delle comunicazioni elettroniche (rifusione)’.
78. Legislative Decree no. 208 of 8 Nov. 2021, ‘Attuazione della direttiva (UE) 2018/1808 del Parlamento europeo e del Consiglio, del 14 novembre 2018, recante modifica della direttiva 2010/13/UE,

IV. Secondary Legislation

56. In the field of media, many detailed provisions are laid down in secondary legislation, which includes decrees of the President of the Republic (*decreti del Presidente della Repubblica*) adopted by the Government, Ministerial Decrees (*decreti ministeriali*) issued by individual Ministries, and decisions (*delibere*) adopted by AGCom.

For instance, sponsored programmes are regulated, *inter alia*, by Ministerial Decree no. 581 of 1993.[80] More recently, AGCom adopted Decision no. 606/10/CONS[81] and Decision no. 607/10/CONS, laying down regulations concerning, respectively, the provision of on-demand AVMS and the provision of linear services on 'other electronic communication networks' (e.g., broadband, mobile networks).

57. AGCom's regulatory powers are expressly set forth in the Maccanico Law[82] and in the CLAVMS.[83] In particular, the Maccanico Law empowers AGCom's Services and Product Committee to adopt implementing regulations in the fields of telecommunications[84] and advertising,[85] in order to fine-tune the balance between the free exercise of those activities and constitutionally protected values such as the protection of viewers.[86] AGCom, moreover, is responsible for the enforcement of rules governing political communication[87] and may adopt regulations to implement those rules.[88]

Several scholars have questioned the constitutionality of AGCom's regulatory powers, insofar as that authority is not accountable to the Parliament or other elected bodies.[89] Other authors, however, have highlighted that the legal basis for AGCom's regulatory powers is set out in primary legislation, thus ensuring compliance with the constitutional principle of *riserva di legge*.[90]

---

relativa al coordinamento di determinate disposizioni legislative, regolamentari e amministrative degli Stati membri, concernente il testo unico per la fornitura di servizi di media audiovisivi in considerazione dell'evoluzione delle realtà del mercato'.

79. Legislative Decree no. 177 of 31 Jul. 2005, as amended by Legislative Decree no. 44 of 15 Mar. 2010 and further amendments, 'Testo unico dei servizi di media audiovisivi e radiofonici' ('Consolidated Law on Audiovisual and Radio Media Services' or 'CLARMS').
80. Decree of the Minister of Communications 9 Dec. 1993, no. 581.
81. As amended by Decision nos 285/21/CONS, 188/21/CONS, 76/21/CONS, 75/21/CONS, 74/21/CONS, 600/20/CONS, 231/20/CONS, 408/19/CONS, 50/19/CONS, 561/18/CONS, 468/18/CONS, 492/17/CONS, 445/17/CONS and 305/17/CONS.
82. *See* Art. 6 of the Maccanico Law.
83. *See* Art. 9 CLAVMS.
84. *See* Art. 1, para. 6, letter (b) no. 3 of the Maccanico Law.
85. *Ibid.*, Art. 1, para. 6, letter (b) no. 5.
86. R. Zaccaria, A. Valastro, E. Albanesi, *Diritto dell'informazione e della comunicazione* (Padua: Cedam, 2021).
87. *See* Art. 1, para. 6, letter (b) no. 9 of the Maccanico Law.
88. *See* Art. 6, para. CLAVMS.
89. N. Marzona, 'Il potere normativo delle autorità indipendenti', in *I garanti delle regole*, ed. S. Cassese, C. Franchini (Bologna: Il Mulino, 1996), 87 et seq.
90. M. Cuniberti, 'Autorità amministrative indipendenti e Costituzione', *Rivista di diritto costituzionale* (2002): 26 et seq.

V. Self-Regulation and Co-regulation

58. Self-regulation is a type of voluntary initiative that enables economic operators, social partners, Non-governmental organizations (NGOs), and associations to adopt common guidelines among themselves and for themselves. Co-regulation, in turn, establishes a legal link between self-regulation and national legislation and typically envisages State intervention in case of non-compliance.

59. The oldest example of self-regulation in the media sector in Italy is the Advertising Self-Regulation Code (*Codice di autodisciplina pubblicitaria*), adopted by the Institute for Advertising Self-Regulation (*Istituto dell'Autodisciplina Pubblicitaria*) in 1966. Since then, the Code has been updated more than sixty times in order to take into account the developments that occurred in the advertising sector.[91] The Code seeks to ensure that advertising complies with certain consumer protection standards. The Code is binding only on its signatories, which include Italy's major advertisers, consultants, and media operators.[92]

60. Regard must be had also to the 'Media and Minors' Self-Regulation Code (*Codice di Autoregolamentazione Media e Minori*).[93] Drafted in 2002 as a self-regulation instrument among broadcasters, the Code acquired co-regulatory status in 2004, when the Gasparri Law required all broadcasters – not only those that had pledged to abide by the Code – to comply with the provisions on the protection of minors set out in said Code. The CLAVMS currently sets out an equivalent requirement.[94]

The CLAVMS also provides that AGCom should rely upon co-regulation procedures to devise the necessary technical arrangements to ensure that minors do not have access to inappropriate content, such as filtering systems and personal identification numbers.[95] AGCom is also entrusted with the task of monitoring compliance with the provisions on the protection of minors, including those set out in the 'Media and Minors 'Self-Regulatory Code, and may impose sanctions on infringers.[96]

61. In 2003, several Internet Service Providers (ISPs) associations as well as the Minister for Communications and the Minister for Innovation and Technologies signed the 'Internet and Minors Code'.[97] The purpose of the Code is to prevent minors from accessing inappropriate content. To this end, the Code sets out some

91. The latest version of the Code is available at: https://www.iap.it/codice-e-altre-fonti/il-codice/.
92. *See* https://www.iap.it/conoscere-iap/associati/.
93. The original denomination of the Self-Regulation Code at issue was 'TV and minors' (*Codice di autoregolamentazione TV e minori*). Following the extension of the regulatory framework also to non-linear services, Art. 6, para. 1, of the Decree of the President of the Republic 14 May 2007, no. 72 changed the name of the Self-Regulation Code to 'Media and Minors'.
94. *See* Art. 37, para. 6, CLAVMS.
95. Article 37, para. 5, CLARMS.
96. In this regard, *see also* Italian Council of State's Judgment No. 2418 of 14 Apr. 2020.
97. Self-Regulation Code 'Internet and minors', signed on 19 Nov. 2003, available at: http://www.privacy.it/archivio/codinternetminori.html.

guidelines for ISPs, including the duty to provide differentiated browsing, classification of conditional access contents, age identification systems and so forth.[98]

62. Finally, it is worth mentioning the Self-regulation Code on the Representation of Court Proceedings in Television Broadcasts,[99] signed in 2009 by the major public and commercial broadcasters, the National Association of Journalists, and the Italian Press Federation. The subscribers pledged to abide by a set of basic principles (objectivity, thoroughness, and impartiality) and to respect human dignity, honour and reputation, as well as the privacy of people directly, indirectly, or occasionally involved in investigations and court proceedings.

VI. Useful Links

63.

- EUR-Lex, official EU legal documents Search Engine: https://eur-lex.europa.eu/.
- Official Journal of the Italian Republic: www.gazzettaufficiale.it/.
- Italian Legislation Search Engine: https://www.normattiva.it/.
- AGCom Decisions Search Engine: https://www.agcom.it/atti-e-provvedimenti.
- Constitutional Court case law: https://www.cortecostituzionale.it/actionPronuncia.do.
- Administrative Courts case law: https://www.giustizia-amministrativa.it/web/guest/dcsnprr.
- Court of Cassation case law: http://www.italgiure.giustizia.it/sncass/.

98. *Ibid.*, Art. 3(2)–(4).

99. Self-regulation Code on the Representation of Court Proceedings in Television Broadcasts (*Codice di autoregolamentazione in materia di rappresentazione di vicende giudiziarie nelle trasmissioni radiotelevisive*), signed on 21 May 2009, available at: https://www.agcom.it/comitato-processi-in-tv.

Part I. Freedom of Speech

§1. The Constitutional Underpinning for the Freedom of Expression: Article 21

64. The freedom of expression is expressly enshrined in Article 21 of the Italian Constitution. That article consists of six paragraphs. The first paragraph contains a broad statement that everyone has the right to express his or her thoughts through any media.

65. The following paragraphs unravel a set of guarantees protecting the means of communication that, at the time the Constitution was drafted, appeared as the most relevant one: the press. In particular, the Constitution provides that the press may not be subject to authorization or censorship; seizure of the press is permitted only for offences expressly set out by the law and on the basis of a reasoned Court order,[100] except in cases of urgency where the timely intervention of the judicial authority is not possible; the law may establish that the financial sources of the periodical publications be disclosed.

Paragraph 7 sets out the only express derogation from the freedom of expression affirmed in paragraph 1: public morals. Printed publications and shows contrary to public morals are prohibited and punished in accordance with the law.

I. The Beneficiaries of the Freedom of Expression

66. The subjective scope of Article 21 is very broad. According to the wording of that provision, the freedom of expression applies to 'everyone', not just to Italian or EU nationals.[101] The Constitutional Court, accordingly, held that the freedom of expression also extends to foreign nationals.[102]

67. Moreover, Article 21 of the Constitution applies both to individuals and groups. The Constitutional Court acknowledged that the freedom of expression can be exercised collectively through companies, associations, and NGOs.[103]

100. Law no. 47 of 8 Feb. 1948.
101. *See* A. Barbera, 'Articolo 2', in *Commentario alla Costituzione,* ed. G. Branca (Bologna-Roma: Zanichelli, 1975), 117 et seq.
102. Constitutional Court, judgment no. 11 of 1968.
103. Constitutional Court, judgment no. 126 of 1985.

Whether public bodies and organizations are entitled to the same degree of freedom of expression is currently debated, as according to Article 97 of the Constitution public powers can be exercised only within the bounds set by the law.

68. Elected officials enjoy a stronger form of freedom of expression, as its exercise contributes to ensuring the functioning of the national political process. According to the Constitution, neither Members of the Parliament[104] nor Members of Regional Assemblies[105] can be held liable for the opinions they express in the performance of their functions. Nevertheless, it is often unclear whether opinions are expressed in the exercise of political functions or outside that context.[106]

II. Forms of Expression Protected by the Constitution

69. Drawing the boundaries of the material scope of Article 21 of the Constitution has proved somewhat arduous. It is, for instance, an open question whether the Constitution also protects spurious forms of expression of thoughts, such as incitement to action.

In its early decisions, the Constitutional Court adopted a conservative approach and held that seditious cries and demonstrations in public places fell outside the scope of Article 21 of the Constitution, so they could legitimately be criminalized.[107]

The Constitutional Court, however, abandoned this approach in subsequent rulings.[108] Most scholars currently favour a broad construction of Article 21 of the Constitution as protecting not only forms of expression related to intellect but also forms of expression linked to emotions,[109] regardless of their guise.[110]

70. Although Article 21, paragraph 1, of the Constitution protects the freedom of expression 'through any other means', it does not follow that individuals enjoy an unfettered right to gain access to the media.

In fact, access to means of information is comprehensively regulated by primary legislation,[111] whose purpose is to ensure that all opinions are afforded equal opportunities to be heard.[112]

104. *See* Art. 68 of the Constitution.
105. *See* Art. 122(4) of the Constitution.
106. *See*, for instance, Constitutional Court, Judgment no. 10 of 2000; Judgment no. 11 of 2000; Judgment no. 304 of 2007; Judgment no. 28 of 2008.
107. Constitutional Court, Judgment no. 120 of 1975; no. 100 of 1996.
108. Constitutional Court, Judgment no. 67 of 1966; no. 84 of 1969; no. 67 of 1966; no. 108 of 1974; no. 67 of. 1966; no. 96 of 1981.
109. P. Barile, *Libertà di manifestazione del pensiero* (Milan: Giuffrè, 1975), 229.
110. C. Esposito, 49; A. Pace e M. Manetti, 'Articolo 21', 57; R. Zaccaria, A. Valastro, E. Albanesi, *Diritto dell'informazione*.
111. Constitutional Court, Judgment no. 225/1974.
112. Constitutional Court, Judgment no. 105 of 1974; no. 94 of 1977; no. 59 of 1960.

§2. THE FREEDOM OF INFORMATION

71. Inextricably linked to the freedom of expression is the freedom of information. The latter has a threefold dimension: active (the right to inform others), passive (the right to be informed), and reflexive (the right to gain access to undisclosed information).

Article 21 of the Constitution expressly protects only the active form, that is, the freedom to inform others.[113] Nevertheless, the Constitutional Court,[114] following the pattern of Article 10 of the ECHR, has extended the constitutional protection also to the passive and reflexive dimensions of the freedom of information. Indeed, both the reception of information and access to information are essential for the proper functioning of a democratic society and for the development of an open political debate.

I. The Active Dimension: The Right to Inform Others

72. The active dimension of the freedom of information entails the right to inform others individually and collectively and to inform specified and unspecified recipients.[115]

The freedom to inform others also includes the right to report (*diritto di cronaca*).[116] Some judgments of the Court of Cassation[117] suggest that the right to report is afforded a stronger protection relative to other forms of expression, insofar as journalists facing defamation charges may rely on specific affirmative defences. In fact, the preferential status accorded to the right to report does not stem from Article 21 of the Constitution (which protects all forms of expression alike) but from the Criminal Code, according to which one cannot be punished for exercising his or her rights.[118] The Constitutional Court endorsed this view.[119]

II. The Passive Dimension: The Right to Be Informed

73. The passive dimension of the freedom of information concerns the right to receive information. The existence of that right is, however, debated:[120] some

113. *See* G. Gardini, *Le Regole dell'Informazione. Verso la Gigabit Society* (Turin: Giappichelli, 2021).
114. Constitutional Court, Judgment no. 25 of 1965; no. 18 of 1966; no. 122 of 1970; no. 175 of 1971; no. 105 of 1972; no. 113 of. 1974; no. 16 of 1981; no. 18 of 1981; no. 225 of 1975; no. 231 of. 1975; no. 826 of 1988; no. 420 of 1994; no. 112 of 1993; no. 466 of 2002.
115. *See* G. Gardini, *Le Regole dell'Informazione. Verso la Gigabit Society* (Turin: Giappichelli, 2021).
116. *See* V. Crisafulli, Problematica della 'libertà d'informazione', *Il Politico* (1964): 286; M. Mazziotti, 'Appunti sulla libertà di manifestazione del pensiero nell'ordinamento italiano', *Scritti in onore di Vezio Crisafulli* (Padova: Cedam, 1985): 521; A. Cataudella, *La tutela civile della vita privata* (Milano: Giuffrè, 1972), 17.
117. *See*, for example, Court of Cassation, Judgment of 31 May 1966, no. 1446; Judgment of 21 Dec. 1967, no. 3003.
118. *See* G. Gardini, *Le Regole dell'Informazione. Verso la Gigabit Society* (Turin: Giappichelli, 2021).
119. Constitutional Court, Judgment no. 175 of 1971.
120. *See* G. Gardini, *Le Regole dell'Informazione. Verso la Gigabit Society* (Turin: Giappichelli, 2021).

authors argue that the right to receive information is protected by Article 21 of the Constitution only in an indirect fashion,[121] whereas others contend that the right to be informed is a full-fledged right bestowed upon individuals.[122] This divergence of perspectives reflects a different understanding of the freedom of information: the former regard freedom as a right serving an individual interest to express one's thoughts; the latter espouse a functionalist conception of the freedom of expression as having a social function and underpinning the political process in a democratic society.[123]

74. The right to be informed, in turn, presupposes media pluralism. The diversity of sources of information and the comprehensiveness and accuracy of information provided significantly affects the right to receive information.[124] Pluralism as a constitutional value developed first in the context of television broadcasting and was later extended to other means of information so as to become one of the pillars of the freedom of information in general.[125]

Pluralism has internal, external and substantial dimensions. Internal pluralism concerns the ability of a given means of information to convey a multitude of different cultural, political, and social views. External pluralism entails the availability of as many information sources as possible, having regard to the current state of technical development. Substantive pluralism entails a level playing field in the context of political communication.[126]

III. The Reflexive Dimension: The Right to Gain Access to Undisclosed Information

75. The last aspect of the freedom of information is the reflexive one, that is, access to information that has not yet been made public. This dimension of the freedom of information, thus, typically covers fact-finding and information-gathering carried out by journalists in the exercise of their profession. In this perspective, the reflexive aspect of freedom is functional to its active dimension, hence it is considered worthy of protection under Article 21 of the Constitution.[127]

Access to unpublished information is of paramount importance in the relationship between individuals and public authorities. Scholarly commentators have argued that Article 21 of the Constitution grants individuals a right of access to

121. *See* A. Pace, M. Manetti, 'Art. 21: la libertà di manifestazione del proprio pensiero', in *Commentario della Costituzione*, eds G. Branca, A. Pizzorusso (Bologna: Zanichelli, 2006), 345 et seq.
122. N. Lipari, 'Libertà d'informare o diritto ad essere informati?', *Dir. radiodiff. Telecom.* (1978): 3 et seq.; C. Gessa, 'Libertà di stampa e disciplina della professione giornalistica', *Il Foro amministrativo*, III (1967): 655 et seq.
123. *See also* G. Gardini, *Le Regole dell'Informazione. Verso la Gigabit Society* (Turin: Giappichelli, 2021).
124. Constitutional Court, Judgment no. 155 of 2002.
125. Constitutional Court, Judgment no. 826 of 1988; no. 420 of 1994.
126. Constitutional Court, Judgment no. 112 of 1993; no. 466 of 2002; *See also* G. Gardini, *Le Regole dell'Informazione. Verso la Gigabit Society* (Turin: Giappichelli, 2021).
127. *See* A. Lojodice, *Contributo allo studio sulla libertà di informazione* (Napoli: Jovene, 1969).

documents held by public administrations, within the limits set by the law.[128] The matter of transparency of administrative action has been first comprehensively regulated by Law no. 241/1990.[129]

IV. Permissible Restrictions on Freedom of Information

76. Just like other freedoms enshrined in the Constitution, the freedom of information must, on some occasions, be balanced against constitutional values of equal importance.[130] This may lead to some restrictions being placed upon the freedom of information.[131]

77. Article 21 of the Constitution only envisages one express limit upon the freedom of information: that of 'public morality' (*buon costume*).[132] As early as 1956, however, the Constitutional Court ruled that other limits on the freedom of expression are 'implied' in the Constitution.[133]

The Court clarified that any such limitation is admissible only if: (i) it pursues a constitutional value of equal importance, and (ii) a careful and accurate balancing exercise of the interests at stake is carried out.[134]

A. Public Morality

78. The scope of the notion of 'public morality' has been widely debated and is currently identified with that of 'sexual modesty' rather than with that of 'social morality'.[135] The latter is a legal concept employed in contract law: contracts that are at variance with the collective social standards embedded in a specific historical and geographical context are null and void.[136] Public morality as sexual modesty is, instead, a concept employed in criminal law, where the protection of the development of the personality of children is the main concern.[137] In this connection, the notion of public morality can be contrasted with that of obscenity, that is, the lack

---

128. A. Valastro, 'Articolo 21', *Commentario alla Costituzione* (Milan: Utet, 2006): 457.
129. Law 7 Aug. 1990, no. 242.
130. *See* A. Pace, M. Manetti, 'Art. 21: la libertà di manifestazione del proprio pensiero', in *Commentario della Costituzione*, eds G. Branca, A. Pizzorusso (Bologna: Zanichelli, 2006), 39 et seq.
131. *See* Constitutional Court, Judgment no. 9 of 1965; no. 120 of 1968; no. 38 of 1973; no. 11 of 1974; no. 106 of 1974; no. 123 of 1976; no. 16 of 1981. *See also* A. Pace, M. Manetti, 'Art. 21: la libertà di manifestazione del proprio pensiero', *Commentario della Costituzione*, ed. G. Branca, A. Pizzorusso (Bologna: Zanichelli, 2006), 100.
132. Constitutional Court, Judgment no. 120 of 1968.
133. Constitutional Court, Judgment no. 1 of 1956.
134. Constitutional Court, Judgment no. 19 of 1962; no. 9 of 1965.
135. Constitutional Court, Judgment no. 9 of 1965; no. 120 of 1968; no. 191 of 1970; no. 49 of 1971; no. 1063 of 1988; no. 487 of 1989.
136. Court of Cassation, Judgment of 7 Jul. 1981, no. 4414.
137. Constitutional Court, Judgment no. 9 of 1965.

of 'sexual modesty and public decency in the public sphere'.[138] In other words, public morality concerns the forms of expression of sexuality that, in a given context, are in keeping with human dignity in its individual[139] and social dimensions.[140]

The notion of public morality under Article 21 of the Constitution, therefore, is narrower than the corresponding contract law notion.[141] Indeed, a broader interpretation of public morality could have triggered an undue restriction of the freedom of expression. Such a narrow interpretation of public morality is also supported by the preparatory work of the Constitution, which clearly show that the drafters preferred the wording *buon costume* over the broader expression *moralità pubblica*.[142]

B. Honour and Reputation

79. Respect for honour and reputation are commonly recognized as implied limits on the freedom of expression. The protection of honour and reputation is linked to the notion of 'social dignity' protected by Article 3, paragraph 1, of the Constitution. 'Honour' can be defined as the perception that everyone has of his or her own value. 'Reputation' is the opinion that others have about a person's value in a given social context.[143]

80. The Constitutional Court has endeavoured to strike a balance between the protection of honour and reputation and the freedom of expression in its various forms. As far as the right to report (*diritto di cronaca*) is concerned, criminal courts have consistently held that reporting facts liable to damage one's honour or reputation is not punishable as long as: (i) there is a public interest underlying the dissemination of those facts; (ii) reported facts are true; and (iii) facts are reported in an appropriate and accurate fashion. In a similar vein, the Court of Cassation in September 2013 ruled that having one's face displayed in the background of a television feature on a Gay Pride parade could not be regarded as harmful to the concerned person's honour and reputation, insofar as being identified abstractly in a crowd in connection with an event of public interest is one of the 'risks of life' no one can avoid.[144]

81. Balancing honour and reputation against the freedom of expression has proven more arduous in the case of criticism. The right to criticize (*diritto di critica*) is the right to express an opinion (often, but not necessarily, a negative one)

138. *See* G. Gardini, *Le Regole dell'Informazione. Verso la Gigabit Society* (Turin: Giappichelli, 2021).
139. Constitutional Court, Judgment no. 368 of 1992.
140. Constitutional Court, Judgment no. 368 of 1992; no. 487 of 1989.
141. Constitutional Court, Judgment no. 9 of 1965; no. 16 of 1965; no. 120 of 1968; no. 49 of 1971; no. 293 of 2000; no. 368 of 1992.
142. *See* P. Barile, *Libertà di manifestazione del pensiero* (Milan: Giuffrè, 1975), 24.
143. G.E. Vigevani, 'Il diritto di cronaca e di critica', *AA.VV., Percorsi di diritto dell'informazione* (Torino: Giappichelli, 2006): 59; *See also* G. Gardini, *Le Regole dell'Informazione. Verso la Gigabit Society* (Turin: Giappichelli, 2021).
144. *See* Court of Cassation, Judgment of 18 Sep. 2013, no. 24110. *See also* Arena, A. 'Court of Cassation Rules on Right to Image in relation to a Gay Pride Parade Television Feature'. IRIS 3 (2014): 32 et seq., available at: https://merlin.obs.coe.int/article/6826.

about a certain fact or person.[145] Unlike the right to report facts (*diritto di cronaca*), the right to criticize entails a subjective understanding of reality; hence, it has been argued that the latter should not be afforded the same affirmative defences against criminal prosecution applicable to the former. Nonetheless, according to the case law, the expression of opinions is not punishable if: (i) opinions are based on true facts;[146] (ii) there is a public interest in the opinion concerned; (iii) opinions are expressed in a suitable and decent manner.[147]

82. Satire involves an exaggerated and surreal representation of reality. Therefore, the possibility to extend to satire the principles applicable to the right to report (*diritto di cronaca*) has proven problematic. Courts have clarified that satire is protected by Article 21 of the Constitution if it: (i) does not contain false statements about the person who is the subject of satire;[148] (ii) does not result in an unrestrained disparagement;[149] (iii) concerns a person known to the general public, so that satire can be of general interest.[150]

If satirical messages are disseminated together with actual journalistic content, then those messages must comply with the requirements applying to the reporting of facts (*diritto di cronaca*).[151]

C. *Personal Identity, Privacy and Other Restrictions*

83. Freedom of expression also must be balanced against the value of personal identity (*identità personale*), that is, the right to a true and fair representation of one's personal details.[152] The protection of personal identity is underpinned by the *generalklausel* in Article 2 of the Constitution, which protects 'inviolable human rights'.

Courts have clarified that personal identity does not imply the right to be represented in accordance with one's self-perception, but only on the basis of ascertainable and objective circumstances.[153] Any violation of the right to personal identity may trigger cease and desist orders, the duty to rectify and the right to monetary compensation.[154] Moreover, Article 617 of the Criminal Code provides that revealing, via any means of information, the content of private conversations or communications is a felony punishable by imprisonment for up to four years. In this

---

145. *See* Court of Cassation, Judgment of 3 Jul. 1993, no. 6493.
146. Court of Cassation, Judgment of 18 Sep. 2008, no. 35646; Trial Court of Rome, Judgment of 3 Feb. 1998.
147. *See* Court of Cassation, Judgment of 15 Jan. 2002, no. 370; Judgment of 20 Nov. 2000, no. 10119.
148. *See* Court of Cassation, Judgment no. 13563 of 1998.
149. Trial Court of Rome, Judgment of 26 Jun. 1993; Trial Court of Trento 26 Jan. 1999.
150. Trial Court of Rome Judgment of 13 Feb. 1992. *See also* M. Mantovani, 'Profili penalistici del diritto di satira', *Diritto dell' Informazione e dell'informatica* (1992): 295.
151. Trial Court of Milan, Judgment of 26 May 1994.
152. *See* Constitutional Court, Judgment no. 13 of 1994; no. 297 of 1996.
153. *See* Constitutional Court, Judgment no. 13 of 1994; *See also* A. Pace, M. Manetti, 'Art. 21: la libertà di manifestazione del proprio pensiero', *Commentario della Costituzione*, ed. G. Branca, A. Pizzorusso (Bologna: Zanichelli, 2006), 132.
154. *See* G. Gardini, *Le Regole dell'Informazione. Verso la Gigabit Society* (Turin: Giappichelli, 2021).

connection, however, the European Court of Human Rights (ECtHR) recently held that a suspended prison sentence of four months and five days imposed by Italian courts on a television presenter for disclosing confidential images of a row involving a famous politician constituted a disproportionate interference with the defendant's freedom of expression.[155]

84. Privacy, albeit not expressly mentioned in the Constitution, constitutes a significant limitation on the freedom of information and in particular on the freedom of the press (*see* below §§ 111–112). The same holds true for national security and the proper functioning of law enforcement, which will be examined in Part II, Chapter 5. Many of the principles developed in case law on the protection of privacy were subsequently incorporated by the legislator in Law no. 675 of 1996. Subsequently, the relevant legislation was codified under the Personal Data Protection Code (PDPC), i.e., Legislative Decree no. 196/2003 as subsequently amended.

155. *See* ECtHR, *Ricci v. Italy*, Appl no. 30210/06 of 8 Oct. 2013. *See also* Voorhoof, D. 'Ricci v. Italy'. IRIS 1 (2014): 1 et seq., available at: http://merlin.obs.coe.int/iris/2014/1/article1.en.html.

Part II. Regulation of Print Media

Chapter 1. The Journalists' Profession

§1. Journalism as a Regulated Profession

85. According to the Journalist Profession Law, a journalist's profession is to report and comment on facts in a truthful and fair manner. That activity, therefore, does not merely consist of the diffusion of news but also is an 'informative intermediation' between the news and the public.[156]

86. Journalism is a regulated profession. Exercising that profession or using the title of journalist without being registered on the Journalists' Roll is a criminal offence punishable by imprisonment for up to six months and a fine.[157]

The Constitutional Court, however, clarified that the registration requirement set out in the Journalist Profession Law does not affect the right vested in every individual to express his or her views through a newspaper.[158] That right stems directly from Article 21 of the Constitution and cannot be restricted by the Journalist Profession Law.[159]

87. Employment contracts entered into between newspapers or periodicals and unregistered journalists are null and void, but the employee is entitled to remuneration and social security benefits for the duration of the employment period.[160]

§2. Categories of Journalists and Entry Requirements

88. The Journalist Profession Law defines three categories of journalists: professional journalists, publicists, and trainees. Publicists and professional journalists

156. *See* G. Gardini, *Le Regole dell'Informazione. Verso la Gigabit Society* (Turin: Giappichelli, 2021).
157. *See* Art. 45 of the Journalist Profession Law (referring to Arts 348 and 498 of the Penal Code).
158. *See* Constitutional Court, Judgment no. 11 of 1968.
159. *See* G. Zagrebelsky, *Questione di legittimità costituzionale della legge 3 febbraio 1963 n. 69 istitutiva dell'Ordine dei giornalisti* (Giurisprudenza Costituzionale, 1968), 311 et seq.; E. Cheli, *In tema di legittimità costituzionale dell'Ordine e dell'Albo dei giornalisti* (Giurisprudenza Costituzionale, 1968), 318 et seq.
160. *See* Court of Cassation, Judgment of 11 Feb. 2011, no. 3385.

must be registered in the respective section of the Roll of Journalists, which is kept, in each Region, by the relevant Board of the Journalists' Council. Trainees are enrolled in a separate Register.

89. Professional journalists practice journalism in an exclusive and continuous manner.[161] The Constitutional Court clarified that professional journalists may carry out other activities, so long as those activities are temporary, occasional, marginal, and ancillary.[162]

Applicants seeking to be registered in the Roll as professional journalists must be of at least 21 years of age, must be enrolled in the Register of trainees, must have completed a traineeship of at least eighteen months, and must have passed a written and oral exam[163] (which also includes the legal provisions applying to journalism).[164] It seems appropriate to point out Article 6 of Law No. 198/2016, which affects the organization of the territorial structure of the Order of Journalists by providing, in addition to the regional and inter-regional ones, also one per 'autonomous province'.

90. Publicists practice journalism on a remunerated and non-occasional basis along with other professions or occupations.[165] Applicants wishing to be entered into the Roll as publicists must show that they have published a certain number of articles (minimum requirements are set by each Regional Board) and that they have worked for a periodical or newspaper for at least two years.[166] Unlike professional journalists, publicists are not required to pass an exam to be entered in the Roll.

91. Trainees can be enrolled in a special Register if they are at least 18 years old and can produce a statement of an editor to the effect that they have started their traineeship.[167] The traineeship must take place at a newspaper, periodical or television editorial section where a certain number of professional journalists are employed.[168] Although trainees cannot be regarded as full-fledged journalists, they are required to abide by journalists' rules of professional ethics.[169]

§3. Electronic Press, Bloggers, and Social Media

92. The proliferation of online newspapers, blogs, and social media has contributed to the pluralism of information enshrined in Article 21 of the Constitution, but

161. *See* Art. 1, para. 3, of the Journalist Profession Law.
162. *See* Constitutional Court, Judgment no. 256 of 1971.
163. *See* Art. 29 of the Journalist Profession Law.
164. Article 32, para. 1, of the Journalist Profession Law.
165. Article 1, para. 4, of the Journalist Profession Law.
166. Article 35, para. 1, of the Journalist Profession Law.
167. Article 33, para. 1, of the Journalist Profession Law.
168. Article 34, para. 1, of the Journalist Profession Law.
169. *See* R. Zaccaria, A. Valastro, E. Albanesi, *Diritto dell'informazione e della comunicazione* (Padua: Cedam, 2021).

at the same time has posed new legal challenges. To what extent should these forms of expression be subject to the same rules applying to journalists and the printed press?

93. Law no. 62/2001 extended some of the rules applying to printed press to electronic publishing by broadening the definition of 'editorial product' set out in the Press Law. That notion currently includes publications recorded on electronic support to be disseminated through electronic means.[170]

94. Therefore, the question arose whether also online newspapers must be enrolled in the Court Register pursuant to the Press Law (Law no. 47/1948).[171] The Court of Cassation held that online newspapers are not subject to the Press law and that the editors of such publications cannot be convicted for failing to enrol them in the Court Register.[172] However, online newspapers and periodicals must comply with the registration requirements if they wish to apply for public financial support.[173]

95. The Maccanico Law requires telecommunication and online service providers to be enrolled in the 'Registry of Communications Operators' (RCO) kept by AGCom. The CLAVMS, in turn, includes online publishing in the 'Integrated Communications System' (ICS), that is, the relevant market defined by the law for the purpose of the application of the anti-concentration thresholds and the ban on dominant positions set out in Article 51 CLAVMS.[174]

96. The Court of Cassation ruled in 2015 that online newspapers enjoy the same constitutional guarantees against seizure as print newspapers,[175] i.e., they can only be subject to seizure in the cases expressly set out by the law, which do not include libellous newspaper stories. Accordingly, the Court of Cassation held that online newspapers featuring those stories cannot be subject to preventive seizure under Article 321 of the Code of Criminal Procedure.[176]

97. In 2016, the Court of Cassation reaffirmed the assimilation between print and online newspapers and observed that the latter can be regarded as instances of 'typographic reproduction' within the meaning of Article 1 of the Press Law. Thus, the Court of Cassation ruled that online newspapers cannot be subject to interim relief

170. Article 1, para. 1 of Law 7 Mar. 2001, no. 62.
171. Law 8 Feb. 1948, no. 47.
172. Court of Cassation, Judgment of 10 May 2012, no. 23230.
173. *Ibid.*, *see also* Art. 7 para. 3 of Legislative Decree no. 70 of 9 Apr. 2003. For scholarly comments, *see* R. Zaccaria, A. Valastro, E. Albanesi, *Diritto dell'informazione e della comunicazione* (Padua: Cedam, 2021), 479 et seq.; F. Bruno, G. Nava, *Il nuovo ordinamento delle comunicazioni. Radiotelevisione, comunicazionioni elettroniche, editoria* (Milan: Giuffrè, 2006), 856 et seq.
174. *See* Art. 3, para. 1, letter (z) CLAVMS.
175. Court of Cassation, Judgment of 17 Jul. 2015, no. 31022.
176. *Ibid.*

measures under the Code of Civil Procedure that have the same effect as seizure or that seek to restrict the distribution of said newspapers.[177]

98. However, the Court of Cassation ruled that newsletters, blogs, fora, newsgroups, mailing lists, chat conversations, and instant messaging cannot be subsumed *en bloc* under the concept of 'press' within the meaning of Article 21 of the Constitution without having regard to their distinctive features. In particular, the Court of Cassation took the view that messages posted on an online forum (which can be public or restricted to members) are similar to handwritten notes pinned to a message board (placed in a public or a private place) which are means of communication but cannot be regarded as 'press' and accordingly are not covered by the constitutional safeguards against seizure.[178]

99. Turning to the status of bloggers, the Court of Cassation held that the right to report and the right to comment stem directly from Article 21 of the Constitution and, as such, they apply not only to journalists[179] but also to anyone wishing to report facts or express opinions by whatever means, including blogs.[180]

100. Finally, the role of social media in policing the limits of the freedom of expression has given rise to considerable debate in recent times, following three controversial court orders concerning the Facebook pages of two extreme-right organizations: CasaPound and Forza Nuova.[181]

101. By its interim order of 12 December 2019, the Commercial Division of the Court of Rome found that Facebook, in view of the number of its users, has a 'special position' that transcends that of a contractual relationship between private parties and is more akin to that of a public service and, for that reason, is bound by the constitutional provisions on pluralism and cannot exclude Casapound from the political debate by taking down its Facebook page.[182]

102. That ruling was upheld by the Commercial Division of the Court of Rome by its order of 29 April 2020, which this time characterized the relationship between Facebook and its users as a contract between private parties, involving a tension between Facebook's right to economic enterprise and the Casapound's right to

177. Court of Cassation, Judgment of 25 Oct. 2016, no. 23469.
178. Court of Cassation, Judgment of 10 Mar. 2009, no. 10535; Judgment of 17 Jul. 2015, no. 31022.
179. Court of Cassation, Judgment of 25 Jul. 2008, no. 31392.
180. *See* Part I, §2, III *supra*.
181. *See* M. Bassini, Libertà di espressione e social network, tra nuovi 'spazi pubblici' e 'poteri privati'. Spunti di comparazione, in *Rivista di Diritto dei Media,* issue 3, 2019, 93–97.
182. *See* A. Arena, Rome Commercial Court enjoins Facebook to reactivate CasaPound Italia's account, in *IRIS*, 2020, 1:1, p. 29; C. Caruso, La libertà di espressione presa sul serio. CasaPound c. Facebook, Atto I, in www.sidiblog.it, 20 Jan. 2020; R. Bin, Casapound vs Facebook : un'ordinanza che farà discutere, in www.lacostituzione.info, 15 Dec. 2019; O. Grandinetti, Facebook vs. CasaPound e Forza Nuova, ovvero la disattivazione di pagine social e le insidie della disciplina multilivello dei diritti fondamentali, in Media Laws, issue 1, 2021.

political speech. *In casu*, the Commercial Division found that Casapound was not an illegal organization and that taking down its Facebook page was therefore unwarranted.

103. Between those two rulings concerning Casapound, the Immigration Division of the Court of Rome issued an order on 23 February 2020 concerning the dispute between Facebook and the extreme-right organization Forza Nuova. On this occasion, the Italian judges found that not only Facebook was entitled to take down Forza Nuova's page, but was in fact required to do so. According to the Immigration Division, Facebook was a private entrepreneur carrying out an activity of undeniable relevance to society, so Facebook's relationship with its users was governed not only by its terms of use but also by the Italian provisions adopted to implement Directive 2009/31/EC on electronic commerce. Thus, Facebook would have been liable if it had failed to take down Forza Nuova's page, as it had become aware of the illegal nature of the content posted on that page.

104. While those conflicting outcomes may be accounted for by the different sensitivities of the Commercial Division and the Immigration Division of the Court of Rome,[183] they certainly call for legislative action on this matter, considering that the legal regime in force dates back to 2003.[184]

183. C. Melzi d'Eril, G.E. Vigevani, Odio in rete e rimozione delle pagine Facebook: giudice che vai, soluzione che trovi, in *Il Sole 24 Ore*, 27 Feb. 2020.
184. M. Bassini, Libertà di espressione e social network, tra nuovi 'spazi pubblici' e 'poteri privati'. Spunti di comparazione, in Rivista di *Diritto dei Media*, issue 3, 2019, at 97.

Chapter 2. Journalists' Rights

§1. Role of Journalists as Watchdogs of Society

105. The Constitutional Court has consistently held that freedom of expression seeks to protect the free flow of information and the pluralism of opinions because they are essential elements for the proper functioning of a democratic polity.[185]

106. With specific reference to the press, the Court of Cassation has ruled that it constitutes a privileged forum for the involvement of public opinion in the political debate taking place within elected bodies.[186] Recalling the European Court of Human Rights (ECtHR) jurisprudence,[187] the Court of Cassation added that newspapers must be regarded as the 'watchdogs' of democratic institutions, including the judiciary.[188]

107. The Court of Cassation also held that the exercise of the right to report and to comment by journalists is to be welcomed insofar as it contributes to monitoring the administration of justice and ensuring that members of the judiciary do not overstep the bounds of their profession.[189]

§2. Journalists' Independence

108. Article 21 of the Constitution seeks to ensure journalists' independence from governmental influence by prohibiting most of the restrictive practices employed by the Fascist regime to control the press.[190] Notably, prior authorization regimes entailing the discretionary power of political and administrative bodies are forbidden, as well as any form of censorship.[191]

Moreover, seizure of press is permitted only for printed materials that have already been published, only in connection with criminal offences for which the Press Law expressly requires seizure (the so-called *riserva di legge*, *see* General Introduction, §3.II.B), and only in the presence of a Court order (the so-called *riserva di giurisdizione*).[192]

---

185. *See* Constitutional Court, judgment no. 1030 of 1988; no. 81 of 1993.
186. *See* Court of Cassation, Judgment of 2 Jul. 2007, no. 25138.
187. *See* ECtHR, *Kobenter and Standard Verlags Gmbh v. Austria*, application no. 60899/00, paras 29 and 30.
188. *See* Court of Cassation, Judgment of 9 Feb. 2011, no. 15447.
189. *See* Court of Cassation, Judgment of 23 Jan. 1984 no. 3743 and Judgment of 21 Feb. 2007 no. 25138.
190. *See* generally P. Caretti, *Diritto dell'informazione e della comunicazione: stampa, radiotelevisione, telecomunicazioni, teatro e cinema* (Bologna: Il Mulino, 2013).
191. *See* Art. 21, para. 2 of the Constitution; *see also* Constitutional Court, Judgment no. 1 of 1956. On the notion of censorship, *see* Constitutional Court, Judgment no. 159 of 1970. As to the ban on prior authorization and censorship, *see* Constitutional Court, Judgment no. 1 of 1956; no. 11 of 1974; no. 115 of 1957; no. 31 of 1957; no. 38 of 1961.
192. *See* Art. 21, para. 3 of the Constitution.

In cases of urgency, when obtaining a Court order is unfeasible, law enforcement agencies can autonomously seize printed publications but must notify the Court having jurisdiction of the seizure.[193] That Court must uphold the seizure within twenty-four hours, otherwise, the seizure becomes ineffective.[194]

109. The bulwark of journalists' independence *vis-à-vis* the bargaining power of publishers is the Journalists' Council.[195]

The Constitutional Court has expressly recognized the Council's role in safeguarding the independence of its affiliates.[196] Some scholarly commentators, however, have voiced doubts about the ability of a body constraining journalists' freedom to effectively safeguard their independence.[197]

110. Journalists' independence from the political leanings of the newspaper they work for is ensured by the so-called Conscience Clause (*clausola di coscienza*), included in the collective agreement entered into between the National Federation of Italian Journalists (*Federazione Nazionale della Stampa Italiana*) and the Italian Federation of Newspaper Publishers (*Federazione Italiana Editori Giornali*).[198]

Under the conscience clause, a journalist is entitled to unilaterally terminate his or her employment relationship, with full economic benefits, in case of a significant shift in the newspaper's political alignment.[199]

§3. Protection of Journalistic Sources

111. The Journalist Profession Law requires journalists and publishers to maintain professional secrecy about the source of the news when it is necessary due to confidentiality of the news.[200] That provision, however, does not expressly state that journalists and editors can lawfully refuse to disclose the identity of their source if so requested by a Court.[201]

112. As the 1930 Code of Penal Procedure did not include journalists among the professionals who could not be required to testify about facts learned in the exercise

193. *See* Art. 21, para. 4 of the Constitution.
194. *See* Art. 21, para. 5 of the Constitution.
195. This clearly emerges from the *travaux préparatoires* of the Journalist Profession Law. *See* M. Rossano, *Configurazione sistematica dell'esercizio della professione giornalistica* (IV Giurisprudenza Costituzionale, 1967), 165.
196. *See* Constitutional Court, Judgment no. 11 of 1968.
197. *See* S. Fois, 'Giornalisti (ordine dei)', *Enciclopedia del diritto,* vol. XVIII (Milan: Giuffrè, 1969), 713.
198. Contratto Nazionale di Lavoro Giornalistico 2013–2016, available at: https://www.fnsi.it/upload/70/70efdf2ec9b086079795c442636b55fb/d162eafd355b3be9d336cb8de89daa00.pdf.
199. *Ibid.*, Art. 32.
200. Article 2, para. 3 of the Journalist Profession Law.
201. *See* A. Pace, M. Manetti, 'Art. 21: la libertà di manifestazione del proprio pensiero', in *Commentario della Costituzione,* eds G. Branca, A. Pizzorusso (Bologna: Zanichelli, 2006), 341–342.

of their job (e.g., lawyers, medical doctors, religious ministers, etc.),[202] journalists could be enjoined to disclose their sources in the course of legal proceedings.

In this respect, the Constitutional Court held that no discrimination existed between journalists and the above professionals and that the freedom of expression under Article 21 of the Constitution should, on some occasions, yield to the pursuit of other constitutional values such as the administration of justice.[203]

113. The current Code of Penal Procedure (1988) expressly provides that registered professional journalists cannot be required to divulge the names of the people from which they obtained confidential information in the exercise of their profession.[204]

That privilege only applies to registered professional journalists (not to publicists and trainees)[205] and covers the name of the informant as well as any information (e.g., telephone numbers)[206] that could lead to his or her identification.[207]

114. The protection of journalistic sources envisaged by the Code of Penal Procedure, however, is qualified by the power vested in courts to enjoin journalists to disclose their sources if the relevant information is indispensable to prove the crime being investigated and if the truthfulness thereof can only be established by identifying the source.[208]

It is apparent from the wording of the Code of Penal Procedure that the said power can be exercised by courts only in exceptional circumstances (e.g., if the informant is the only witness who can prove the innocence of the defendant).[209]

Some scholars have argued that the criminal courts' power to enjoin journalists to reveal the identity of their sources cannot be extended, by way of analogy, to civil courts.[210]

202. *See* Art. 351 of the Code of Penal Procedure (1930).
203. Constitutional Court, Judgment no. 1 of 1981.
204. *See* the first sentence of Art. 200, para. 3, of the Code of Penal Procedure (1988).
205. But *see* P. Caretti, *Diritto pubblico dell'informazione* (Bologna: Il Mulino, 1994), 64 (criticizing that limitation).
206. *See* Court of Cassation, Judgment of 21 Jan. 2004, no. 22397.
207. *See* Court of Cassation, Judgment of 16 Feb. 2007, no. 25755.
208. *See* the last sentence of Art. 200, para. 3, of the Code of Penal Procedure (1988).
209. *See* A. Pace, M. Manetti, 'Art. 21: la libertà di manifestazione del proprio pensiero', *Commentario della Costituzione,* ed. G. Branca, A. Pizzorusso (Bologna: Zanichelli, 2006), 344.
210. *Ibid.*, 343.

Chapter 3. Journalists' Liability

§1. General Information on the Liability System

115. The two main forms of liability under Italian law are contractual and non-contractual liability. Contractual liability is governed by Article 1218 of the Civil Code, which provides that if a debtor fails to duly or timely perform his or her obligation, the debtor must compensate the creditor unless such failure or delay is attributable to circumstances beyond the debtor's control.

Contractual liability often arises from a contractual obligation, but it can just as well stem from an obligation flowing from other sources, such as unjust enrichment, *negotiorum gestio*, and so forth.[211]

To escape contractual liability, the debtor must show that he or she acted with an ordinary diligence or, in the case of professionals, the average diligence required for that particular job or profession.

As per Article 1228 of the Civil Code, if the debtor takes advantage of the work of third parties in discharging his or her obligations, the debtor is liable for the conduct of those parties.

116. Non-contractual liability, akin to tort liability in Common law jurisdictions, is set out in Article 2043 of the Civil Code, according to which whoever, either intentionally or out of negligence, causes unjust harm to another person is legally bound to compensate that person.

Unlike contractual liability, non-contractual liability does not stem from a specific preexisting obligation, but from a general obligation not to harm others (*neminem laedere*). Typically, non-contractual liability can result from the commission of a criminal offence, such as defamation or libel. Parties harmed by the commission of a criminal offence can choose whether to bring their non-contractual liability claim before the criminal Court dealing with that criminal offence or to bring a separate claim before a civil Court.

The burden of proof in case of non-contractual liability rests on the harmed party, who must show that the other party acted negligently or intentionally caused the harm.

While the culpability of the wrongdoer is usually a precondition for non-contractual liability, the Civil Code also envisages cases of strict liability. For instance, under Article 2049 of the Civil Code, patrons and owners are liable for the harm caused by their helpers and employees in the performance of their tasks. The Court of Cassation clarified that a plaintiff claiming a violation of Article 2049 of the Civil Code is not required to prove that the patron or owner has been negligent in selecting (*culpa in eligendo*) or supervising (*culpa in vigilando*) his or her employees,[212] but only the existence of an employment relationship and that the offending conduct was related to the employee's tasks.[213]

211. *See* Court of Cassation, Judgment of 26 Jun. 2007, no. 14712.
212. Court of Cassation, Judgment of 3 Aug. 2001, no. 10705.
213. Court of Cassation, Judgment of 20 Jun. 2001, no. 8381.

§2. Is There a Special Liability Regime for Journalists? Who Will Be Held Liable: Only the Journalist or Also the Publisher?

117. As to the liability of journalists, the case law has set some legal limits to their right to report and comment (*diritto di cronaca e di critica*).[214] In particular, the Court of Cassation delivered a landmark ruling (known as the 'Decalogue Ruling') summarizing the three requirements that must be met for the exercise of freedom of the press not to give rise to liability: (i) the diffusion of the news must be socially useful; (ii) the reported facts must be true, and (iii) the representation and assessment of facts must be sober and fair. Those requirements will be examined seriatim.[215]

118. The social utility criterion implies that the right to report and comment can only lawfully encroach upon other rights, such as the right to privacy, if it can contribute to the formation of public opinion about facts of objective relevance for society as a whole.[216]

119. The truthfulness criterion is expressly recognized as one of the basic duties of the journalistic profession by Law no. 69/63.[217] The notion of 'truthfulness' requires correspondence between events as they are reported by the journalist and events as they actually occurred.[218] Mere verisimilitude does not meet the truthfulness requirement.[219] Accordingly, journalists are under an obligation to carefully and diligently check their sources.[220] Reported news, moreover, must also be comprehensive, as an incomplete account of a fact could substantially distort or misrepresent its significance.[221]

120. The fair representation and comment criterion implies that the exercise of the freedom of the press must neither go beyond the goal to inform the audience nor cause harm to the reputation of the persons concerned. The Court of Cassation, in particular, took the view that this criterion is not met when journalists employ subterfuges such as skilful innuendos, evocative juxtapositions or a disproportionately outraged tone.[222]

---

214. *See*, for example, Court of Cassation, Judgment no. 5941 of 2000; no. 747 of 2000; no. 8035 of 1998; no. 2113 of 1997; no. 40415 of 2004.
215. *See* Court of Cassation, Judgment no. 5259 of 1984. On the doctrine on the limits to the exercise of the right to report news and the case law of the Court of Cassation, *see also* G.E. Vigevani, *Libertà di espressione, onore e controllo del potere. Sviluppi del diritto di critica politica, tra giudice nazionale ed europeo*, in *Percorsi costituzionali* 2015, pp. 67–84.
216. *See* Court of Cassation, Judgment no. 1473 of 1998.
217. *See* Art. 2 of Law no. 69 of 1963.
218. *See* Court of Cassation, Judgment no. 5491 of 2000.
219. *See* Court of Cassation, Judgment no. 8848 of 1997.
220. *See*, for example, Court of Cassation, Judgment no. 2173 of 1993; no. 5259 of 1984; no. 7747 of 1997.
221. *See*, for example, Court of Cassation, Judgment no. 5259 of 1984; no. 1904 of 2003.
222. *See* Court of Cassation, Judgment no. 5259 of 1984.

121. The Court of Cassation subsequently added a fourth requirement, that is, the timeliness of the news.[223] This requirement rests on the recognition of the so-called right to be forgotten:[224] even if the facts reported are true and accurate, every person has the right not to be indefinitely exposed to further discomfort or embarrassment as it may result from the repeated publication of facts lawfully disclosed at an earlier time. In those cases, it is necessary to determine whether there is a renewed or ongoing public interest in learning about facts reported at an earlier time.

With regard to the right to be forgotten, in recent years, there has been a strong debate on the breadth of its protection under Italian law. That right has emerged in the case law as a peculiar expression of the right to privacy and takes into account the interest of a subject to return to anonymity after abandoning the activity from which he or she had derived notoriety.[225]

122. Following the ruling of the ECJ in *Google Spain,*[226] the right to be forgotten was expressly recognized at the EU level by the General Data Protection Regulation (GDPR) in 2017.[227] Article 17 of the GDPR entitles data subjects to obtain from the data controller the erasure of personal data concerning them without undue delay. In order to ensure the consistency of Italian legislation with the right to be forgotten provisions of the GDPR, Legislative Decree no. 101/2018 amended the relevant parts of the PDPC.

123. Turning to the responsible editor's liability for the defamatory articles written by journalists under his or her supervision, the Press Law clearly provides that in case of libel, the author of the article and the editor are jointly and severally liable to provide compensation.[228] In addition to the ordinary civil liability, the Press Law provides that journalists convicted of libel must also make financial reparation to the victim in accordance with the seriousness of the insult and the diffusion of the

223. *See* Court of Cassation, Judgment no. 3679 of 1998. *See also* Trial Court of Bari, Judgment of 27 Sep. 2008 (holding that making an article published at an earlier time available through an online database does not infringe the right of privacy or the right to be forgotten).
224. But *see* A. Pace, M. Manetti, 'Art. 21: la libertà di manifestazione del proprio pensiero', *Commentario della Costituzione,* ed. G. Branca, A. Pizzorusso (Bologna: Zanichelli, 2006), 133–134 (arguing that the demand not to write about a particular subject has an 'inherently censorial content' and that a full-fledged right to be forgotten has no clear legal basis in Italian law).
225. *See* Trial Court of Rome, Judgment of 3 Dec. 2015, no. 23771. *See* G.M. Riccio, *L' esordio del diritto all'oblio nella giurisprudenza italiana,* in *Il diritto dell'Informazione e dell'Informatica,* 2016, pp. 271 et seq.
226. ECJ Judgment of 13 May 2014, *Google Spain SL and Google Inc. v Agencia Española de Protección de Datos (AEPD) and Mario Costeja González,* Case C-131/12, EU:C:2014:317.
227. Regulation (EU) 2016/679 of the European Parliament and of the Council of 27 Apr. 2016 on the protection of natural persons with regard to the processing of personal data and on the free movement of such data, and repealing Directive 95/46/EC (General Data Protection Regulation).
228. Article 11 of the Press Law.

offending article.[229] Courts are divided over the issue of whether also newspaper editors must provide such an additional reparation.[230]

§3. Defamation and Libel

124. The category of press offences followed an evolutionary path. During the Fascist era, the authoritarian ethos of criminal law favoured the proliferation of press offences. As a consequence, many conducts allegedly detrimental to the personality of the State, to religious sentiments and to public order were criminalized.

Following the entry into force of the Constitution in 1948, the legislature, often prompted by the Constitutional Court, decriminalized most of those conducts, except for the ones impinging upon the rights of individuals, such as insult and defamation.[231]

125. The defamation offence set out in Article 595 of the Penal Code punishes the conduct of harming another person's reputation while communicating with other people.

That crime is only punishable if the victim reports it to law enforcement agencies or the judiciary; the latter cannot bring defamation charges *motu proprio*.

The penalty for defamation is imprisonment from six months to three years or a fine of not less than EUR 516. The victim can also bring an autonomous compensation claim. Every year a significant number of judgments are delivered on compensation claims related to libel cases.

126. Under the Press Law, libel (*diffamazione a mezzo stampa*) is punishable by imprisonment from one to six years and a fine.[232] The criminal responsibility rests both on the author of the offending article and on the responsible editor if the latter failed to carry out the necessary supervision to prevent the libel.[233] Accordingly, all newspapers and periodicals are required to appoint a responsible editor.[234]

It has been alleged that the responsible editor's duty of supervision could lead to a form of censorship contrary to Article 21 of the Constitution. The Constitutional Court, however, rejected that claim. According to the Court, the notion of 'censorship' only includes powers of *ex ante* control entrusted to public authorities, not the

229. Article 12 of the Press Law.

230. *See* Court of Cassation, Judgment of 5 Mar. 2010, no. 13198 (holding that not only the author of the offending article, but also anyone who contributed to the libel or failed to prevent it must provide the victim with the additional reparation set out in the Press Law); but *see* Trial Court of Rome, Judgment of 6 Jul. 2004 (holding that the responsible editor of a newspaper must not provide the victim with the additional reparation set out in the Press Law unless it is established that he or she aided and abetted the author of the offending article).

231. *Ibid.*, 55. *See also* G. Gardini, *Le Regole dell'Informazione. Verso la Gigabit Society* (Turin: Giappichelli, 2021).

232. Article 13 of the Press Law.

233. Article 57 of the Penal Code (stating that the editor is subject to the penalty imposed on the author of the article reduced up to one-third).

234. Article 3, para. 1 of the Press Law.

supervision tasks carried out by editors. Those tasks, indeed, constitute the very essence of an editor's profession, not only a legal requirement to avoid criminal responsibility in libel cases.[235]

§4. Privacy and Data Protection

127. The protection of privacy may constitute a limit on the freedom of the press.[236] In the absence of an express reference in the Constitution, the right of individuals not to have their privacy encroached upon by external interference is usually believed to have a basis in Article 2 of the Constitution, which reads as follows: 'The Republic recognizes and guarantees the inviolable rights of the person'. The Constitutional Court first endorsed that view in 1975.[237] The right to privacy is also related to other freedoms protected by the Constitution, such as the inviolability of private dwellings enshrined in Article 14 of the Constitution and the confidentiality of correspondence set out in Article 15 of the Constitution.[238] The same holds true for the right to personal liberty laid down in Article 13 of the Constitution and the sanctity of family affirmed in Article 29 thereof. The Constitutional Court has also referred to Article 3, which, in protecting citizens' social dignity, postulates a sphere of autonomy from external interference.[239]

128. The main item of Italian legislation dealing with privacy is the PDPC, whose enforcement is entrusted to the Personal Data Protection Authority (PDPA). The necessity to strike a balance between press freedom and the right to privacy prompted the adoption of specific rules on the processing of personal data carried out in the context of journalism.[240] A Code of ethics on the processing of data in the context of journalism was adopted in 1998[241] and attached to the PDCP as Annex A.1. Following the entry into force of Legislative Decree no. 10/2018, designed to bring the PDPC in line with the GDPR, the above Code of ethics was replaced by the Rules of ethics on the processing of personal data in the context of journalism,[242] which currently constitute Annex A of the PDPC.

129. Particular regard must be had to the provisions set out in Article 6 of the Rules of ethics, according to which the disclosure of facts, even in detail, of significant public or social interest is allowed when it is necessary to describe how a given event took place or to characterize its actors. Failure to comply with that and

235. Constitutional Court, Judgment no. 44 of 1960, para. 3.
236. *See*, for example, Court of Cassation, Judgment no. 4487 of 1956; no. 31991960; no. 990 of 1963; no. 38 of 1973; no. 868 of 1974; no. 2199 of 1975; no. 5658 of 1998 and 8889 no. 2001.
237. *See* Court of Cassation, Judgment no. 2199 of 1975.
238. *See* M. Cuniberti, *supra* n. 89, 123.
239. *See* Constitutional Court, Judgment no. 29 of 1975.
240. *See* R. Zaccaria, A. Valastro, E. Albanesi, *Diritto dell'informazione e della comunicazione*, (Padua: Cedam, 2021); D. Piccione, *Diritto di cronaca giornalistica dei parlamentari e pubblicazioni delle intercettazioni telefoniche a loro carico* (Giurisprudenza costituzionale, 2008), 1573 et seq.
241. https://www.garanteprivacy.it/home/docweb/-/docweb-display/docweb/1556386.
242. https://www.garanteprivacy.it/web/guest/home/docweb/-/docweb-display/docweb/9067692.

the other provisions of the Rules of Ethics may prompt the PDPA to prohibit the processing of data.[243]

243. Article 145, para. 5, PDPC.

Chapter 4. Right to Reply

§1. The Constitutional Underpinning of the Right to Reply

130. The right of reply was considered by the drafters of the Constitution and of the Press Law as the bulwark against possible abuses of the freedom of the press. Accordingly, the Press Law enshrined a broad and unconditional version of that right.[244]

131. The Constitutional Court held that the right of reply under the Press law had a twofold constitutional underpinning: the protection of a 'fundamental right of individuals'[245] and the pursuit of a 'public interest to the objectivity of information'.[246] The latter argument, however, appears to clash with the deference inherent in the Press Law to the subjective assessment of the person seeking to exercise the right of reply.[247]

132. Recent jurisprudence and scholarly writings, accordingly, regard the safeguard of personal dignity and identity as the true constitutional underpinning of the right of reply under the Press Law.[248] The pursuit of the pluralism of information, therefore, is a mere by-product of the exercise of the right of reply,[249] which cannot be considered an autonomous expression of thoughts protected by Article 21 of the Constitution.[250]

§2. The Right to Reply under Primary Legislation

133. The Press Law (Law no. 47 of 1948) requires newspapers and periodicals to publish free of charge a reply or statement by whoever deems that such a newspaper or periodical disclosed images or reported facts or statements that the person concerned deems false or detrimental to his or her dignity.[251]

---

244. *See* A. Pace, M. Manetti, 'Art. 21: la libertà di manifestazione del proprio pensiero', *Commentario della Costituzione*, eds G. Branca, A. Pizzorusso (Bologna: Zanichelli, 2006), 792–793.
245. Constitutional Court, Judgment no. 225 of 1974.
246. Constitutional Court, Judgment no. 133 of 1974.
247. *See* Court of Cassation, Judgment of 22 Jun. 1985, no. 3769.
248. *See* A. Pace, M. Manetti, 'Art. 21: la libertà di manifestazione del proprio pensiero', *Commentario della Costituzione,* eds G. Branca, A. Pizzorusso (Bologna: Zanichelli, 2006), 794.
249. *See* Court of Cassation, Judgment of 5 Apr. 1990, no. 2852.
250. *See* A. Pace, M. Manetti, 'Art. 21: la libertà di manifestazione del proprio pensiero', *Commentario della Costituzione,* eds G. Branca, A. Pizzorusso (Bologna: Zanichelli, 2006), 794; But *see* E. Roppo, 'Il diritto di rettifica nella disciplina dei mezzi di comunicazione di massa', *Foro Italiano,* I (1983): 463 and S. Di Palma, 'Forma e sostanza del diritto di rettifica', *Foro Italiano,* I (1990), 3457 (arguing that Art. 21 is the constitutional underpinning of the right of reply).
251. Article 8, para. 1 of the Press Law.

The reply or statement must refer to the offending article and must be published in full, so long as they do not exceed thirty lines of text[252] and they do not contain statements that may lead to a criminal conviction.[253]

Daily newspapers must publish the above reply at the top of the same page where the offending article appeared and no later than two days from the request of the person concerned.[254] Periodicals must publish the above reply on the same page as the offending article no later than two issues from the week the reply request is received.[255] Failure to comply with the right of reply within the above deadlines was decriminalized in 1981[256] but may still give rise to an interim Court order enjoining the publication of the reply[257] as well as to the imposition of an administrative fine.[258]

134. The right of reply also applies to media service providers as per Article 35 CLAVMS. Anyone who deems that his or her legitimate interests, in particular reputation and good name, have been damaged by an assertion of incorrect facts in a television programme may request that the relevant media service provider exercises the right of reply.[259] The reply shall be transmitted within forty-eight hours of the request in a time slot and in a manner equivalent to those of the offending broadcast.[260] Failure to comply with that deadline may result in a complaint being lodged with AGCom, which may enjoin the AVSM provider to broadcast the reply within twenty-four hours of its decision.[261]

135. Legislative Decree no. 188/2021,[262] implementing Directive 2016/343 on the strengthening of certain aspects of the presumption of innocence,[263] introduced a special procedure for the exercise of the right of reply *vis-à-vis* public statements made by public authorities that refer to suspects or accused persons as being guilty prior to their conviction.[264] Those persons may request the authority that made such statements to correct them.[265] The corrected statement must be published within forty-eight hours of the request in a manner equivalent to that of the offending statement.[266] Should the public authority fail to comply with this duty, the person

252. Article 8, para. 4 of the Press Law.
253. Article 8, para. 1 of the Press Law.
254. Article 8, para. 2 of the Press Law.
255. Article 8, para. 3 of the Press Law.
256. *See* Art. 8 of Law 5 Aug. 1981, no. 416, OJIR 6 Aug. 1981, no. 215.
257. Article 8, para. 5 of the Press Law.
258. Article 8, para. 6 of the Press Law.
259. Article 35, para. 2, CLAVMS.
260. Article 35, para. 3, CLAVMS.
261. Article 35, para. 4, CLAVMS.
262. Legislative Decree no. 188 of 8 Nov. 2021.
263. Directive (EU) 2016/343 of the European Parliament and of the Council of 9 Mar. 2016 on the strengthening of certain aspects of the presumption of innocence and of the right to be present at the trial in criminal proceedings.
264. Article 2, para. 1, of Legislative Decree no. 188 of 8 Nov. 2021.
265. Article 2, para. 2, of Legislative Decree no. 188 of 8 Nov. 2021.
266. Article 2, paras. 3 and 4, of Legislative Decree no. 188 of 8 Nov. 2021.

concerned may seek an injunction against the public authority from Civil Courts under Article 700 of the Code of Civil Procedure.[267]

267. Article 2, para. 5, of Legislative Decree no. 188 of 8 Nov. 2021.

Chapter 5. Access to Public Information

§1. Public Documents and Meetings

136. The right to publish documents by public entities is an important indicator of the true democratic character of a given legal system. In this connection, regard must be had to documents covered by the so-called secret of State.

137. The Constitutional Court ruled that the secret of State is not incompatible with the Constitution, insofar as it is designed to protect national security as per Article 126 of the Constitution.[268]

The scope of the secret of State has been recently clarified by Law no. 124 of 2007.[269] According to Article 39 thereof, the secret of State covers all acts, documents, facts, and activities whose disclosure may undermine the integrity, independence and defence of the State, its relations with other States, or the functioning of State institutions and bodies of constitutional relevance. Some scholars have argued that that definition oversteps the boundaries set by the Constitutional Court as to the permissible scope of the secret of State.[270]

138. Article 261 of the Penal Code provides that the disclosure of information covered by the secret of State is punishable by imprisonment of at least five years. The penalty is increased if the disclosure takes place during wartime if it hinders the military power of the State, and if it is carried out with political or military espionage purposes. Those penalties also apply to those who obtain such information.

139. Article 262 of the Penal Code criminalizes the disclosure of news that the competent authority required not to be made public. Disclosing and obtaining such news is punishable by at least three years of imprisonment.

The wording of this provision could be construed as granting public authorities a boundless power to prohibit the disclosure of news. The Constitutional Court, however, clarified that the news covered by Article 262 of the Penal Code are akin to those covered by the secret of State, in that: (i) they must concern a State interest of compelling importance; and (ii) their disclosure must be such as to appreciably undermine that interest. The characterization of a given piece of information as 'classified' by public authority does not automatically trigger Article 262 of the Penal Code: it is for courts to determine on a case-by-case basis whether the two requirements above are met.[271]

140. Article 202 of the Code of Penal Procedure requires public servants not to testify about circumstances covered by the secret of State. It is for the relevant Court

268. *See* Constitutional Court, Order no. 49 of 1977; Judgment no. 82 of 1977; no. 86/1977.
269. Law 3 Aug. 2007, no. 124.
270. P. Pisa, *Le premesse 'sostanziali' della normativa sul segreto di Stato*, ed. M. Chiavario, Segreto di Stato e giustizia penale, (Bologna:1978), 37.
271. *See* Constitutional Court, Judgment nos 282/1990, 333/1991 and 295/2002.

to seek confirmation from the President of the Council of Ministers as to whether a given matter is covered by the secret of State. If the President provides such confirmation and the classified matter is essential for proving the crime being investigated, the defendant must be acquitted due to the existence of a secret of State. If the President does not provide such confirmation within sixty days, the Court requires the witness to testify over the relevant matter.

§2. Court Hearings and Documents

I. Investigative Secrecy and the Publication of Court Documents

141. The publication of Court documents, especially those concerning pretrial investigations, involves a balancing exercise between, on the one hand, citizens' right to be informed about Court cases and journalists' role as watchdogs of society and, on the other hand, the course of justice is not perverted by undue information leaks.

In this connection, the Constitutional Court has ruled that some Court documents can be subject to investigative secrecy (*segreto istruttorio*) and that it is up to the legislature to strike a balance between the freedom of expression and the administration of justice.[272]

142. Investigative secrecy is governed by Article 329 of the Code of Penal Procedure. Documents and reports by the Public Prosecutor or by law enforcement agencies are subject to investigative secrecy until the defendant is entitled to access those documents and, in any case, until the completion of pretrial investigations.[273]

For investigative purposes, the Public Prosecutor may consent to the publication of specific documents covered by investigative secrecy[274] and may forbid the publication of documents not subject to investigative secrecy.[275]

143. The rules concerning the publication of Court documents are set out in Article 114 of the Code of Penal Procedure. Paragraph 1 thereof proscribes the publication, also in part or in summary form, of investigation documents covered by investigative secrecy as well as of their contents.

Investigation documents not subject to investigative secrecy can be published only after the completion of pretrial investigation. Their contents, instead, can be published at all times.

---

272. *See* Constitutional Court, Judgment no. 25 of 1965. For commentaries, *see* V. Crisafulli, *In tema di limiti alla cronaca giudiziaria* (Giurisprudenza costituzionale, 1965), 245; V. Barosio, *Il divieto di pubblicare atti o documenti relativi ad una istruzione penale e la sua compatibilità con gli artt. 3 e 21 Cost.* (Giurisprudenza costituzionale, 1966), 176. More recently L. Garlati, G.E. Vigevani (eds), *Processo e informazione*, Milano: Giuffré 2012.
273. Article 329, para. 1, of the Code of Penal Procedure.
274. Article 329, para. 2, of the Code of Penal Procedure.
275. Article 329, para. 3, of the Code of Penal Procedure.

144. If the trial reaches the hearing stage, Court documents can only be published, in whole or in part, after the judgment is delivered. In the case of closed-door hearings,[276] instead, Court documents can only be published ten years after the final judgment is rendered and upon authorization by the Minister of Justice. The identity and image of minors involved in criminal proceedings as witnesses or victims cannot be disclosed until they reach the age of eighteen. It is also forbidden to publish images depicting the defendant in handcuffs or other restraints unless the defendant consents to the publication.

145. In 2009 the Press Council, the National Federation of Italian Journalists, and a number of major national and local broadcasters signed a Self-Regulation Code concerning the representation of Court proceedings in television broadcasting.[277] The enforcement of that Code has been entrusted to an ad hoc Committee and to the Press Council.

II. The Publication of Wiretap Transcripts

146. Wiretap transcripts are among the most sensitive Court documents. The monitoring of private conversation constitutes a significant encroachment upon the freedom of communication enshrined in Article 15 of the Italian Constitution. Wiretapping, however, is also a valuable instrument for the detection and suppression of crimes.

The Constitutional Court, accordingly, has repeatedly called upon the legislature to determine when and how wiretaps can take place and to ensure judicial review.[278] The legislature, in turn, enacted several items of legislation to regulate wiretapping.[279]

147. The publication of wiretap transcripts has given rise to a lively political and legal debate. The Constitutional Court has cautioned against the reckless publication of wiretap transcripts involving elected officials as undue means of political pressure.[280] The Italian Data Protection Authority has repeatedly urged journalists to adopt a more cautious approach in publishing wiretap transcripts of famous people or elected officials as doing so could significantly undermine their right to privacy.[281] In this regard, it is worth reminding the ECtHR ruling no. 25337/94 of

276. *See* Art. 472, paras 1 and 2, of the Code of Penal Procedure.
277. Available at: https://www.odg.it/testo-unico-dei-doveri-del-giornalista/24288.
278. *See* Constitutional Court, Judgment no. 34 of 1973. *See also* Judgment no. 366 of 1991; no. 63 of 1994; no. 463 of 1994; no. 372 of 2006.
279. *See*, for example, Law 8 Apr. 1974, no. 98; Art. 240 and Arts 266–271 of the Code of Penal Procedure; Law 20 Jun. 2003, no. 140 (Art. 6 of that law was declared unconstitutional in Judgment no. 390 of 2007 of the Constitutional Court; Law 20 Nov. 2006, no. 281).
280. Judgment no. 390 of 2007.
281. *See* Personal Data Protection Authority, Decision of 21 Jun. 2006, 'Publishing Transcripts of Tapping Records', available in English at: https://www.garanteprivacy.it/web/guest/home/docweb/-/docweb-display/docweb/1299615.

17 July 2003, on the dissemination in the press of wiretap transcripts obtained during a trial against Bettino Craxi, and ruling no. 22765/12 in February 2015 on a case involving Romania. The Government in 2008 proposed an outright ban on the publication of wiretap transcripts (the so-called Alfano Bill),[282] but the bill was eventually dropped in view of the strong opposition of the public opinion and of the concerns raised by some academic commentators as to the consistency of the bill with the Constitution and the ECHR.[283]

148. The matter of the publication of wiretaps transcripts was addressed by Legislative Decree No. 216/2017, which introduced Article 617 *septies* of the Criminal Code, punishing with imprisonment up to four years the disclosure of fraudulent recordings of private meetings, but enabling the disclosure of such recordings if it takes place in the context of court proceedings. Moreover, the above Legislative Decree introduced Article 114, paragraph 2*bis*, of the Code of Criminal Procedure, which introduced an outright ban – whose infringement is a misdemeanour under section 684 of the Criminal Code – on the publication, in whole or in part, of the contents of the wiretaps not acquired in line with the relevant provisions of the Code of Criminal Procedure.[284]

149. Moreover, Law 281 of 2006 grants a remedy to people harmed by the publication of the contents of illegal wiretapping (i.e., carried out in the absence of a Court order): the publisher and the responsible editor are jointly and severally liable up to EUR 0.50 for each printed copy of the offending article or up to EUR 1 million if the transcripts were disclosed through radio, television, or the internet.[285]

---

282. Chamber of Deputies, Legislative Proposal no. 1415, submitted by the Minister of Justice Mr Angelino Alfano on 30 Jun. 2008, available at: www.camera.it/_dati/leg16/lavori/stampati/pdf/ 16PDL0005770.pdf.

283. *See* F. Ruggieri, *Il disegno di legge governativo sulle intercettazioni: poche note positive e molte perplessità* (Cassazione penale, 2008), 2239 et seq.; L. Della Corte, R. Paudice, I. Vozzo, *La disciplina delle intercettazioni (DDL Alfano) alla luce del principio della libertà di espressione garantita dalla Carta Costituzionale e dalla Convenzione Europea dei Diritti dell'Uomo,* report of the research group directed by Prof. R. Mastroianni presented on 15 Jul. 2009, available at: www.odg.it/files/ Rapporto%20contro%20Alfano.pdf.

284. The prohibition applies to wiretaps not acquired pursuant to Articles 268, 415-bis or 454 of the Code of Criminal Procedure.

285. Law 20 Nov. 2006, no. 281.

Chapter 6. Press Council

§1. The Press Council: National Board and Regional Boards

150. The Press Council (*Ordine dei Giornalisti*) was established in 1925,[286] but its prerogatives over the Journalists' Roll were soon devolved to the Press Union, set up by the Fascist regime as a part of the so-called Corporative State with a view to controlling the press and repressing political dissent among journalists.[287]

Following the entry into force of the Constitution in 1948, in order to promote the freedom of expression that had hitherto been constrained by the regime, a provisional procedure was put into place to liberalize access to the journalist's profession.[288]

151. It was only in 1963 that, at the request of journalists, the Parliament passed the Journalist Profession Law, which remodelled the Press Council and restored its exclusive competence to keep the Journalists' Roll.

The Press Council consists of twenty Regional Boards (one for each Italian Region) and a National Board.

152. Regional Boards are composed of six professional journalists and three publicists elected by the professional journalists and publicists registered in the Journalists' Roll kept by that Board.[289] Regional Board Members remain in office for three years and can be re-elected.[290]

Apart from keeping the Journalists' Roll, Regional Boards are responsible for the enforcement of the Press Law and of rules of professional ethics and for instituting disciplinary actions against offending members.[291] Regional Boards, moreover, may bring legal proceedings against people exercising the journalist's profession or using that title without being registered in the Roll.[292]

153. The National Board of the Journalists' Council is established within the Ministry of Justice and it is composed of no more than sixty members, two-thirds of whom are professionals and one-third freelance journalists, elected by the members of the regional and inter-regional Associations, with at least one representative of recognized linguistic minorities in each category. Candidates for the National Council must have an active social security position with the National Welfare Institution for Italian Journalists (INPGI).[293]

---

286. Law 31 Dec. 1925, no. 2307, *Disposizioni sulla stampa periodica.*
287. *See* Royal Decree 26 Feb. 1928, no. 384.
288. *See* P. Murialdi, *La stampa italiana del dopoguerra 1943–1972* (Roma: Laterza, 1973), 157.
289. Article 3 of the Journalist Profession Law.
290. Article 7 of the Journalist Profession Law.
291. Article 11, para. 1, letters (a) and (d) of the Journalist Profession Law.
292. Article 11, para. 1, letter (b) of the Journalist Profession Law.
293. Article 16 of the Journalist Profession Law.

Members of the National Board hold office for three years and can be re-elected.[294] No one can be a Member of the National Board and of a Regional Board at the same time.[295]

The National Board is responsible for coordinating Regional Boards, providing non-binding opinions on legislative proposals concerning the journalist's profession, and hearing appeals against decisions by Regional Boards concerning registration and disciplinary matters.[296]

§2. Journalists' Professional Ethics Between Self-Regulation and Co-Regulation

154. The Journalist Profession Law grants the Press Council a broad discretion in the establishment and enforcement of rules of professional ethics. Article 2 thereof sets out a broad statement that journalists are entitled to report and to comment within the limits set by the law and by the need to protect personal identity. Journalists, moreover, are under an unconditional obligation to uphold the truth and to act in a dutiful and fair manner. Article 48 of the Journalist Profession Law empowers Regional Boards to institute disciplinary proceedings against journalists who engage in conduct unfit for the dignity and repute of the profession or harmful to their own reputation or that of the Press Council.

155. In view of the vague wording of the said provisions of the Journalist Profession Law, the Press Council has endeavoured to flesh out those provisions by adopting a number of self-regulatory and co-regulatory instruments.[297]

156. The Treviso Charter,[298] first adopted in 1991 by the Press Council and the National Federation of Italian Press and updated in 1995 and 2006, lays down guidelines to ensure that journalists act in a manner consistent with the proper development of minors. The Treviso Charter is expressly referred to in Article 7 of the Ethics Code concerning data processing in the journalist's profession (*see* below).

157. The Charter of Journalists' Duties[299] was proclaimed by the Press Council and the National Federation of Italian Press in 1993 with the aim of laying down a number of rules of professional ethics whose violation may lead to disciplinary action. On 1 January 2021, the Single text on the duties of journalists[300] came into

294. Article 17, para. 1, of the Journalist Profession Law.
295. Article 18, para. 1, of the Journalist Profession Law.
296. Article 20, para. 1. Letters (a), (b), and (d) of the Journalist Profession Law.
297. A brief description of the major self-regulatory and co-regulatory instruments is available at: https://www.odg.it/etica.
298. Available at: https://www.odg.it/allegato-2-carta-di-treviso/24290.
299. Available at: https://www.odg.it/testo-unico-dei-doveri-del-giornalista/24288.
300. Available at: https://www.odg.it/testo-unico-dei-doveri-del-giornalista and related amendments available at: https://www.odg.it/wp-content/uploads/2020/11/Modifiche-al-TU-giornalisti_19_11_20-.pdf.

force. It was drawn up in response to the need to harmonize the previous deontological documents in order to provide greater clarity of interpretation and to facilitate the application of all the rules, non-compliance with which may result in the member's disciplinary liability. This act incorporates the contents of the following documents: the Charter of the Duties of Journalists; the Charter of the Duties of Journalists in Press Offices; the Charter of Duties of Economic Information; the Florence Charter; the Milan Charter; the Perugia Charter; the Rome Charter; the Treviso Charter; the Information and Advertising Charter; the Information and Polls Charter; the Code of Ethics relating to Journalistic Activities; the Code on the Representation of Judicial Events in Radio and Television Broadcasts; and the Decalogue of Sports Journalism.

158. To reconcile journalistic activity with the requirements of privacy law, a Code of ethics on the processing of data in the context of journalism was adopted in 1998[301] and attached to the PDCP as Annex A.1. The above Code of ethics was replaced by the Rules of ethics on the processing of personal data in the context of journalism,[302] which currently constitute Annex A of the PDPC.

§3. Disciplinary Sanctions and Proceedings

159. Article 51 sets out four categories of sanctions that Regional Boards may impose, by way of a reasoned decision, upon journalists: (i) warning; (ii) censure; (iii) suspension from the Roll from two months to one year; (iv) debarment. Warnings are given in case of minor infringements of the rules of professional ethics.[303] Censure is a formal rebuke for a violation of the said rules.[304] Suspension can be imposed if the journalist acted in a manner so as to harm his or her professional dignity.[305] Debarment can take place only if the journalist's conduct seriously impaired his or her professional standing so as to make his or her registration in the Roll incompatible with the dignity of the profession.[306]

160. A journalist subject to a disciplinary action is entitled to be heard by the Board as well as to submit written observations and documents. Disciplinary measures are adopted by secret vote and must be fully reasoned.[307]

The decisions of the local Journalists' Board concerning entry into or deletion from the register and in disciplinary matters may be challenged by the person concerned and by the competent public prosecutor by lodging an appeal with the National Board within thirty days.[308]

301. https://www.garanteprivacy.it/home/docweb/-/docweb-display/docweb/1556386.
302. https://www.garanteprivacy.it/web/guest/home/docweb/-/docweb-display/docweb/9067692.
303. Article 52 of the Journalist Profession Law.
304. Article 53 of the Journalist Profession Law.
305. Article 54 of the Journalist Profession Law.
306. Article 55 of the Journalist Profession Law.
307. Article 57 of the Journalist Profession Law.
308. Article 60 of the Journalist Profession Law.

Part III. Regulation of Audiovisual Media (Broadcasting)

Chapter 1. Public Service Broadcasting

§1. The Concept and Mission of Public Service Media

161. The entrustment of PSM tasks in Italy was not carried out, as generally required by the EU legislation in the field of public procurement, through a public tender,[309] but rather through a direct conferral of those tasks to Italy's former broadcasting monopolist, RAI-Radiotelevisione Italiana S.p.A. (hereinafter: 'RAI'). Article 59, paragraph 1, CLAVMS entrusts the operation of PSM to RAI and Article 63(1) CLAVMS sets 30 April 2027 as the expiry date of the PSM concession. The following paragraphs of Article 63 CLAVMS set out a procedure for the award of the PSM concession for a period of ten years.

162. PSM in Italy can be regarded as a set of specific duties – the PSM remit[310] – in the framework of the general interest duties all media providers must comply with. Although the definition of broadcasting as a 'public utility in the general interest' was coined by the Constitutional Court in 1960 to justify State monopoly over that activity,[311] this 'general interest' language is used nowadays also with reference to commercial operators. Article 6, paragraph 1, CLAVMS emblematically stipulates that 'the provision of information through AVMS constitutes a service of general interest' and is accordingly subject to a number of horizontal obligations (the truthful presentation of facts and events, the obligation to broadcast news programmes every day, the duty to grant access to all political subjects, etc.). Moreover, other sets of provisions of the CLAVMS, such as the rules on short news

---

309. But *see* Judgment of the Court of First Instance of 26 Jun. 2008, *SIC – Sociedade Independente de Comunicação, SA v. Commission of the European Communities* Case T-442/03 [2008] ECR II-01161 (holding that Portuguese Republic was 'in no way' required to organize a competitive tendering prior to entrusting PSM tasks to RTP). On the necessity of awarding PSM obligations on the basis of competitive tendering, *see* R. Mastroianni, 'Public Service Media and Market Integration: A Differential Application of Free Movement and State Aid Rules?', in *Market Integration and Public Services within the EU*, ed. M. Cremona (Oxford: Oxford University Press, 2011), pp. 167–169.
310. *See* Article 59, paragraph 2 CLAVMS.
311. Constitutional Court, Judgment no. 59 of 1960.

reports and the promotion of European works, entrust commercial audiovisual media service providers with general interest duties which are, to some extent, akin to those conferred upon the PSM.

163. Just as the commercial audiovisual media service providers are required to comply with a number of obligations in the general interest, the company entrusted with PSM is also allowed to carry out commercial activities other than its public service remit, provided that these additional activities do not interfere with its PSM duties and contribute to ensuring a balanced management of the company.[312]

164. The PSM remit is outlined in Articles 59 and 60 CLAVMS as a number of minimum goals the PSM operator has to meet. Those requirements include: the transmission of programmes of general interest on the whole national territory; an appropriate number of hours, also during prime time, devoted to education, information, cultural promotion through cinema, theatre and musical works; access to programming to political parties, trade unions, religious groups and other associations of social interest; programming destined to be broadcast abroad to promote the knowledge of Italian language and culture; protection of historical archives of radio and television programmes; broadcasting in minority languages; measures to protect people with disabilities; long-distance teaching; interactive digital services.

165. The PSM remit is specified in greater detail in a 'service contract' (*contratto di servizio*) renewed every five years between the PSM operator and the Ministry of Economic Development.[313] Prior to each renewal, the Ministry of Economic Development and AGCom jointly issue guidelines setting out the contents of further PSM obligations to take into account changes in the market and technical context, as well as in the cultural needs of the national and local audience.[314] Moreover, the Parliamentary Supervision Committee (PSC) must give its opinion on the draft public service contract prior to its conclusion.[315] The current service contract for the years 2018–2022 – still in force – was published on 7 March 2018.[316]

166. The CLAVMS lays down both an internal and external supervision system to monitor the PSM operator's compliance with its remit.

As to internal supervision, pursuant to Article 63(9) CLAVMS, RAI's Board of Directors, apart from being the body of the company responsible for all its strategic decisions, is also responsible for ensuring and guaranteeing correct fulfilment of the PSM goals and obligations. The Board of Directors recently adopted an Ethics Code, in March 2020, which expressly mentions the principles of pluralism and impartiality among RAI's 'Ethical basis and objectives'; the task of monitoring

312. Article 59, para. 8, CLAVMS.
313. Article 59, para. 6, CLAVMS.
314. *Ibid* .
315. Article 63, para. 5, CLAVMS.
316. https://www.rai.it/dl/doc/1607970429668_Contratto%20di%20servizio%202018-2022.pdf.

compliance with the provisions of the Code is entrusted to the Standing Committee for the Code of Ethics, which reports to the Managing Director.[317]

The external supervision tasks are, instead, assigned to two different institutions: AGCom and the PSC, which will be examined in Part V below.

§2. THE ORGANIZATION OF PUBLIC SERVICE BROADCASTING

167. RAI is a public company subject to Italian company law.[318] As with other public companies, RAI is governed by three bodies: the Shareholders' General Meeting, the Board of Directors and the Board of Auditors. With reference to Rai's governing bodies, the last major regulatory overhaul was carried out by Law 28 December 2015, no. 220.

168. Nowadays, according to Article 63, paragraphs 15 and 16 of CLAVMS, the Board of Directors consists of seven members: two elected by the Chamber of Deputies and two by the Senate of the Republic, with a vote limited to one candidate; two designated by the Council of Ministers, on the proposal of the Minister for the Economy and Finance; one designated by the RAI employees' assembly. The CEO is appointed by the Board of Directors, on the proposal of the Shareholders' General Meeting.

169. In the past, concerns have been voiced both by scholarly and institutional commentators as to the ability of RAI's governance system to ensure its independence from political and governmental influence. In particular, the Parliamentary Assembly of the Council of Europe, in its Resolution 1387 (2004), underscored that RAI 'has always been a mirror of the political system of the country'[319] and that it 'has moved from the proportionate representation of the dominant political ideologies in the past to the-winner-takes-all attitude reflecting the present political system'.[320]

§3. THE FINANCING OF PUBLIC SERVICE BROADCASTING

170. The PSM operator is financed through a dual-funding system, in that its revenues include both remuneration for commercial activities (notably the sale of advertising space) and compulsory licence fees (*canone di abbonamento*) levied on all owners of television sets.[321] The amount of the latter is set every year in accordance with a decree issued by the Minister of Economic Development.[322] The

317. https://www.rai.it/dl/doc/1586535485463_Codice%20Etico%20_%20Marzo%202020.pdf.
318. Article 63, para. 8, CLAVMS.
319. Parliamentary Assembly of the Council of Europe, Resolution 1387 (2004) adopted on 24 Jun. 2004, *Monopolisation of the electronic media and possible abuse of power in Italy.*
320. *Ibid.*
321. *See* generally C. Schepisi, 'Televisioni e aiuti di Stato: il finanziamento del servizio radiotelevisivo pubblico e gli aiuti per il passaggio al digitale terrestre', AIDA (2010): 48 et seq.
322. Article 61, para. 3, CLAVMS.

licence fee dates back to the 1930s and is still regulated by Royal Legislative Decree no. 246/1938 and by Legislative Decree no. 458/1944. In order to address the issue of fee evasion, the Italian legislature has overhauled the collection system: Article 1(153) of Law no. 208 of 28 December 2015 provides that the possession of a television set, which triggers the obligation to pay the licence fee, can be presumed from the existence of an electricity supply contract. This has paved the way for the collection of the licence fee in the form of a surcharge in the electricity bill.

171. The basic rules for the PSM funding are set forth in Article 61 CLAVMS and include the principle that the licence fee can be employed exclusively to comply with the PSM remit, not to engage in commercial activities. To this end, CLAVMS lays down a separate accounting requirement: in particular, RAI is required to draw up its balance sheet in accordance with a prospectus approved by AGCom in its Decision no. 186/05/CONS[323] as amended by Decision no. 541/06/CONS.[324] The scope of the duties stemming from Article 61 CLAVMS was clarified by the Council of State, which ruled that the above provision precluded RAI from employing its resources to promote Tivù, a joint venture between RAI and Italy's major commercial free-to-air broadcasters, whose corporate mission was to retransmit programmes by its parent companies and third parties on its DTT and satellite networks employing a proprietary encoding protocol.[325]

172. The constitutional justification of the licence fee has been the subject of several rulings by the Constitutional Court.[326] While in the past the licence fee constituted a form of commercial consideration for the services provided by RAI, nowadays it is regarded as a purpose tax (*imposta di scopo*), whose aim is to allow the PSM operator to carry out its remit. Indeed, the Constitutional Court observed that a system of funding based exclusively on advertising revenues would force the PSM operator to take account of audience shares and to adapt its programming to that of its competitors, thus disregarding the PSM remit.[327]

173. Doubts have been expressed by legal scholars as to the effectiveness of the current PSM funding system to fully ensure the independence of the PSM operator from political and governmental influence.[328] As explained above, the amount of the PSM operator's licence fee is set, every year, by a member of the Government, the Minister of Economic Development, so as to cover the costs associated with the fulfilment of the PSM remit for the current year, as can be inferred from the previous

323. Decision no. 186/05/CONS.
324. Decision no. 541/06/CONS.
325. *See* Council of State, Judgment of 20 Aug. 2013, no. 4336. *See also* A. Arena, Council of State Upholds RAI's Obligation to Provide Programmes Free-to-air to all Distribution Platforms. IRIS 10 (2013): 31 et seq., available at: http://merlin.obs.coe.int/iris/2013/10/article31.en.html.
326. *See* Constitutional Court, Judgment nos 248 of 2002 and 155 of 2002.
327. Constitutional Court, Judgment no. 284/02.
328. *See* R. Mastroianni, *Riforma del sistema radiotelevisivo italiano e diritto europeo* (Turin: Giappichelli 2004), 83.

budget, taking into account the prospective inflation rate, and the needs of technological development.[329]

329. *See* Art. 61, para. 3, CLAVMS.

Chapter 2. Private Broadcasting

174. Following the implementation of the AVMSD, the CLAVMS and its implementing acts apply to all providers of AVMS and radio services subject to Italian jurisdiction.[330] AVMS include: 'television broadcasts' (linear AVMS), 'on-demand services' (non-linear AVMS), and 'audiovisual commercial communications'.[331] Those three subcategories will be examined seriatim.

175. 'Television broadcasts' (i.e., linear AVMS) are characterized by the simultaneous viewing of programmes on the basis of a programme schedule set by the media service provider.[332]

176. 'On-demand services' (i.e., non-linear AVMS) are characterized by the viewing of programmes at the moment chosen by the user and at his or her individual request on the basis of a catalogue of programmes selected by the media service provider.[333]

177. 'Audiovisual commercial communications' are images, with or without sound, which are designed to promote, directly or indirectly, the goods, services or image of a natural or legal person pursuing an economic activity; such images accompany, or are included in, a programme or user-generated video in return for payment or for similar consideration or for self-promotional purposes. Forms of audiovisual commercial communication include, *inter alia*, television advertising, sponsorship, teleshopping and product placement.[334]

§1. Different Categories of Private Audiovisual Media Service Providers

178. The CLAVMS contains references to several different categories and subcategories of 'media service providers'.

179. A 'media service provider' is the natural or legal person who has editorial responsibility for the choice of the audiovisual content of the AVMS and determines the manner in which it is organized.[335]

180. The CLAVMS also envisages the notion of 'audiovisual media service providers having a community character', that is, media service providers having editorial responsibility for programme schedules intended for local audiences who undertake to transmit original self-produced programmes for at least half of their

330. *See* Art. 2, para. 1 CLAVMS.
331. Article 3, para. 1, letter. (b) CLAVMS.
332. Article 3, para. 1, letter. (p) CLAVMS.
333. Article 3, para. 1, letter. (q) CLAVMS.
334. Article 3, para. 1, letter. (oo) CLAVMS.
335. Article 3, para. 1, letter (d) CLAVMS.

daily transmission time between 7 am and 9 pm and to broadcast no more than 5% of advertising for each hour of airtime.[336]

181. 'Radio broadcasters' are the holders of an analogue or digital terrestrial radio broadcasting concession or authorization having editorial responsibility for programme schedules falling under any of the three following subcategories: (i) 'radio broadcasters having a community character', (ii) 'radio broadcasters having a local commercial character', or (iii) 'nationwide radio broadcasters'.[337]

182. A 'video-sharing platform provider' is the natural or legal person who provides a 'video-sharing platform service',[338] which in turn is a service whose primary purpose is the provision of programmes, user-generated videos, or both to the general public, for which the video-sharing platform provider has no editorial responsibility, in order to inform, entertain or educate, by means of electronic communications networks. The organization of the service is determined by the video-sharing platform provider, including by automatic means or algorithms, in particular by displaying, tagging and sequencing.[339]

183. The CLAVMS does not define the notion of 'on-demand media service providers', but that of 'on-demand media services', which, as noted above, are AVMS characterized by the viewing of programmes at the moment chosen by the user and at his or her individual request on the basis of a catalogue of programmes selected by the media service provider.[340]

184. Having regard to the vertical structure of electronic communication networks, the CLAVMS further distinguishes between 'network operators', 'media service providers' and 'providers of interactive or conditional access services'. A 'network operator' is the subject entitled to instal, operate, and provide an electronic communications network on digital terrestrial broadcasting frequencies, via cable or satellite.[341] A 'media services provider', as noted above, is the natural or legal person who has editorial responsibility for the choice of the audiovisual content of the AVMS and determines the manner in which it is organized; that notion does not include 'network operators', which only engage in the transmission of programmes falling within the editorial responsibility of third parties;[342] finally, a 'provider of interactive or conditional access services' provides the public or other operators with: (i) conditional access services via the distribution of numerical access keys that enable the viewing of programmes, the billing of services, and the provision of related equipment; (ii) information society services; or (iii) electronic programme guides.[343]

---

336. Article 3, para. 1, letter (r) CLAVMS.
337. Article 3, para. 1, letter (hh), points 1–3 CLAVMS.
338. Article 3, para. 1, letter (l) CLAVMS.
339. Article 3, para. 1, letter (c) CLAVMS.
340. Article 3, para. 1, letter (q) CLAVMS.
341. Article 3, para. 1, letter (f) CLAVMS.
342. Article 3, para. 1, letter (d) CLAVMS.
343. Article 3, para. 1, letter (u) CLAVMS.

§2. Licensing Requirements

185. Prior to the switchover to the digital standard, which took place in 2012, radio and television analogue broadcasting was supposed to be exercised on the basis of concessions. However, operators engaging in analogue broadcasting without a broadcasting concession but in line with other legal requirements were allowed to carry on their activity until the switchover. The de facto exercise of broadcasting activities and the occupation of broadcasting frequencies by operators without a broadcasting concession has been tolerated by Italian broadcasting legislation for several years.[344] However, in 2008, the ECJ established that failure by the Italian Government to free up broadcasting frequencies and to allocate them to legitimate right holders on the basis of objective, transparent, non-discriminatory, and proportionate criteria was inconsistent with the freedom to provide services and the EU electronic communications directives.[345]

186. Nowadays, and until the adoption of the national plan for the allocation of frequencies for analogue radio broadcasting,[346] analogue private radio broadcasting at the national and local levels on national and local terrestrial frequencies is still exercised on the basis of a concession or an authorization[347] by subjects legitimately operating in possession of different requirements in relation to their legal nature, depending on their local, national or European dimension.[348]

187. As to digital broadcasting, the CLAVMS provides different authorization schemes. The provision of AVMS on digital terrestrial frequencies is conditional upon a prior authorization issued by the Ministry of Economic Development,[349] on the basis of the rules set out in AGCom's Digital Broadcasting Regulation.[350]

To be eligible, applicants must: (i) be undertakings established in the European Economic Area or in a Third-country complying with the principle of reciprocity;[351] (ii) have as their objects the exercise of television broadcasting, information, or related activities; (iii) have a share capital and a number of employees greater

---

344. For instance, the Maccanico Law enabled the 'de facto users' of radio frequencies, authorized to carry on their activity under the earlier system, to continue broadcasting on a transitional basis; Decree-Law of 24 Dec. 2003, no. 352 authorized the channels in breach of the concentration thresholds to continue their broadcasts pending the completion of an inquiry into the development of digital television channels; the Gasparri Law extended, by a general authorization mechanism, the possibility for the channels in breach of the threshold to continue to broadcast on the terrestrial radio frequencies until the national allocation plan for radio frequencies for digital television was implemented.
345. ECJ, Judgment of 31 Jan. 2008, *Centro Europa 7 Srl v. Ministero delle Comunicazioni e Autorità per le garanzie nelle comunicazioni and Direzione generale per le concessioni e le autorizzazioni del Ministero delle Comunicazioni,* Case C-380/05, ECR 2008 Page I-00349.
346. The national plan for the allocation of analogue radio broadcasting will be adopted pursuant to the procedure set out in Article 50 CLAVMS.
347. Article 21, para. 1, CLAVMS.
348. Article 21, para. 1, letters (a), (b), (c), CLAVMS.
349. Article 14, para. 1, CLAVMS.
350. *See* AGCom Decision no. 353/11/CONS (AGCom Digital Broadcasting Regulation), as subsequently amended.
351. *Ibid.,* Art. 3, para. 2.

than the minimum requirements set out in the Digital Broadcasting Regulation;[352] (iv) ensure the broadcasting of programmes bearing the same trademark for at least twenty-four hours every week. Public entities, State-controlled companies, and credit institutions cannot either directly or indirectly hold the authorization concerned.[353]

The broadcasting authorization is valid for twelve years, is renewable, and can be transferred to third parties with the assent of the Ministry of Economic Development, in consultation with AGCom.[354] That authorization becomes void upon reaching the expiry date as well as upon its holder's relinquishment, its subjection to bankruptcy procedures or its forfeiture of the relevant subjective or objective requirements.[355]

Holders of the authorizations above are required to pay a fee for the processing of their authorization application;[356] to update a register of programmes on a monthly basis;[357] to preserve complete recordings of the programmes they broadcast for a period of three months;[358] to ensure the right of reply;[359] and to comply with the rules on advertising, sponsorship, teleshopping, and product placement laid down in the CLAVMS and in AGCom's implementing decisions.[360]

188. The provision of linear audiovisual media or radio services through other electronic communication networks (e.g., live streaming, IPTV, web-TV, etc.) is subject to authorization granted by AGCom in accordance with the rules set out in its Decision no. 606/10/CONS.[361]

To be eligible, applicants must: (i) be companies, foundations, or associations established in the European Economic Area or in a State ensuring full reciprocity;[362] (ii) have as their objects the exercise of broadcasting, information, or related activities;[363] (iii) not be represented or administered by persons convicted for crimes punishable by imprisonment of more than six months.[364] Public entities, State-controlled companies, and credit institutions cannot directly or indirectly hold the authorization concerned.[365] Applicants must pay a fee for the processing of their application.[366]

352. *Ibid.*, Art. 3, paras 4 and 5 (requiring a share capital of EUR 6.2 million and at least twenty employees for nationwide broadcasting and a share capital of EUR 155,000 and at least four employees for local broadcasting).
353. *Ibid.*, Art. 3, para. 3.
354. *Ibid.*, Art. 6, para. 1.
355. *Ibid.*, Art. 6, paras 2 and 3.
356. *Ibid.*, Art. 7, para. 1.
357. *Ibid.*, Art. 8, para. 1.
358. *Ibid.*, Art. 8, para. 2.
359. *Ibid.*, Art. 9.
360. *Ibid.*, Art. 10.
361. *See* Attachment A to AGCom Decision no. 606/10/CONS.
362. *Ibid.*, Art. 3, para. 2.
363. *Ibid.*, Art. 3, para. 4.
364. *Ibid.*, Art. 3, para. 3.
365. *Ibid.*, Art. 3, para. 4.
366. *Ibid.*, Art. 6.

Applications for authorization must be deemed successful unless AGCom expressly rejects them within thirty days from the submission of the application.[367] Those authorizations are valid for a period of twelve years and can be renewed and transferred to third parties.

AGCom may withdraw such authorizations if a subject falling short of the relevant subjective and objective requirements acquires control of a company to which such authorizations have been granted.[368] Those authorizations are automatically revoked if: (i) the company holding the authorization is subject to bankruptcy or other insolvency procedures; (ii) one or more authorization requirements are no longer met; (iii) no application for renewal has been submitted by the authorization's expiration date.[369]

189. The exercise of the activity of network operators on terrestrial frequencies, as well as on cable and satellite networks, is subject to the general authorization scheme as per Article 11 of the Electronic Communications Code.[370] That authorization is valid for a period ranging between ten and twelve years and renewable for a period of equal duration.[371]

The general authorization scheme is based on a system of *ex post* control. Undertakings wishing to carry out the activity of network operators must notify the Ministry of Economic Development of a notice stating their intention to do so.[372] Those undertakings can start carrying out their activities immediately.

The Ministry of Economic Development checks ex officio whether the relevant requirements are met and may, within sixty days from the notification of the notice, enjoin the undertakings concerned to suspend their activities.[373] In the case of network operators, eligible applicants must be established in the European Economic Area or in another State ensuring full reciprocity.[374]

General authorizations can be transferred to third parties following notification to the Ministry of Economic Development. The latter may object to that transfer within sixty days of that notification.[375]

190. Providers of interactive and conditional access services are also subject to the general authorization scheme laid down in Article 11 of the Electronic Communications Code.[376]

367. *Ibid.*, Art. 3, para. 8.
368. *Ibid.*, Art. 7, paras 1 and 2.
369. *Ibid.*, Art. 7, para. 3.
370. Article 13, para. 1 CLAVMS.
371. Article 13, para. 3 CLAVMS.
372. Article 11, para. 3, of the Electronic Communications Code.
373. Article 11, para. 7, of the Electronic Communications Code.
374. Article 16, para. 2, of AGCom Digital Broadcasting Regulation.
375. *Ibid.*, Art. 25, para. 8.
376. Article 28 CLAVMS.

Those providers must comply with the technical standards set by AGCom and in particular, those designed to prevent minors from viewing inappropriate content[377] (e.g., filtering systems and personal identification numbers).[378]

Within sixty days from the granting of a general authorization, the provider of interactive and conditional access services concerned must adopt a service charter and submit it to AGCom for approval. That charter is also binding on the provider of programmes and on the network operator that distributes them.[379]

Providers of interactive and conditional access services that are also holders of an authorization to provide linear audiovisual content on terrestrial frequencies must adopt a system of separate accounting for each authorized activity.[380]

191. On-demand service providers are subject to the general authorization scheme too.[381] The undertakings concerned must notify AGCom of the start of their activities, unless AGCom resolves, within thirty days, to enjoin them to stop.[382]

To be eligible, applicants must: (i) be companies, foundations, and associations established in the European Economic Area or in a State ensuring full reciprocity;[383] (ii) have as their objects the exercise of broadcasting, information, or related activities;[384] (iii) not be represented or administered by persons convicted for intentional crimes punishable by imprisonment of more than six months.[385] Applicants must pay a fee for the processing of their application.[386]

The general authorizations above are valid for a period of twelve years, can be renewed and be transferred to others by notifying AGCom of the transfer.[387]

377. Article 15, para. 2, letter (a) of AGCom Digital Broadcasting Regulation.
378. Article 37, para. 5, CLAVMS.
379. Article 15, para. 3 of AGCom Digital Broadcasting Regulation.
380. *Ibid.*, Art. 15, para. 4.
381. Article 19, para. 1 CLAVMS.
382. Article 3, para. 2, of Attachment A to AGCom Decision no. 607/10/CONS.
383. *Ibid.*, Art. 3, para. 3.
384. *Ibid.*, Art. 3, para. 4.
385. *Ibid.*, Art. 3, para. 5.
386. *Ibid.*, Art. 6.
387. *Ibid.*, Art. 5.

Chapter 3. Programme Standards

§1. Impartiality

192. The impartiality, objectivity, fairness, and comprehensiveness of information are, as per Article 4 CLAVMS, general principles of the Italian regime for audiovisual and radio media services.

193. According to Article 6 CLAVMS, one of the aims of that legal framework is to ensure that all political actors may have access to news programmes and political advertising on a non-discriminatory and impartial basis.

194. Those matters are comprehensively regulated by Law no. 28 of 2000[388] and by AGCom Decisions nos 22/06/CSP[389] and 200/00/CSP,[390] which will be examined in Chapter 4 below.

§2. Cultural Diversity

195. The protection of ethnic diversities and of cultural, artistic and natural heritage at the national and local level constitutes a pillar of Italy's AVMS legislation, as per Article 4(1) CLAVMS. That statement is fleshed out by a number of provisions designed to promote the distribution and production of 'European works',[391] as defined in the CLAVMS in line with the AVMSD, and of 'cinematographic works of original Italian expression', as defined by a Ministerial Decree.[392]

196. The CLAVMS lays down *transmission time* quotas and sub-quotas to promote, respectively, European works and works of original Italian expression.[393]

197. Commercial providers of linear AVMS must reserve: (i) a majority proportion of their transmission time (excluding the time allotted to news, sports events,

388. Law 22 Feb. 2000, no. 28, as amended by Law 6 Nov. 2003, no. 313, Legislative Decree no. 104 of 2 Jul. 2010 and Law 23 Nov. 2012, no. 215.
389. AGCom Decision no. 22/06/CSP, 'Disposizioni applicative delle norme e dei principi vigenti in materia di comunicazione politica e parità di accesso ai mezzi di informazione nei periodi non elettorali'.
390. AGCom Decision no. 200/00/CSP, 'Disposizioni di attuazione della disciplina in materia di comunicazione politica e di parità di accesso ai mezzi di informazione nei periodi non elettorali'.
391. For a definition of 'European works', *see* Article 3, para. 1, letter (nn), CLAVMS.
392. Decree of the Ministry of Economic Development and the Ministry of Cultural Heritage and Activities of 22 Feb. 2013. *See also* Arena A., Ministerial Decree Sets Transmission Time and Investment Quotas for Italian Works, IRIS 4 (2013): 20 et seq., available at: http://merlin.obs.coe.int/iris/2013/4/article20.en.html.
393. Article 53 CLAVMS.

games, advertising, teletext services and teleshopping) for European works;[394] (ii) at least one-third of that quota for works of original Italian expression, regardless of their place of production.[395]

The PSM provider must reserve: (i) a quota equal to the majority proportion of its transmission time (as defined above) for European works;[396] (ii) a sub-quota of at least 50% of the previous quota for works of original Italian expression, regardless of their place of production;[397] (iii) a quota equal to at least 12% of its transmission time, in the time slot between 6 pm and 11 pm, to works of fiction, animation, and original documentaries of original Italian expression, regardless of their place of production;[398] (iv) a sub-quota of at least 25% of the previous quota for cinematographic works of original Italian expression, regardless of their place of production.[399]

198. The CLAVMS also sets out *investment* quotas and sub-quotas to promote, respectively, European works and works of original Italian expression.

Commercial providers of linear AVMS must reserve at least 12.5% of their net annual revenues for the production, financing, and purchasing of European works created by independent producers;[400] those providers must also reserve a sub-quota of at least 3.5% of their annual net revenues to cinematographic works of original Italian expression, produced anywhere by independent producers.[401]

199. For the PSM operator, the investment quota for European works is 17% of its net annual revenues, including both revenues from the sale of advertising and from compulsory licence fees;[402] within that quota, the PSM operator must also reserve: (i) a sub-quota of at least 4.2% of its net annual revenues for cinematographic works of Italian origin, produced anywhere by independent producers;[403] (ii) a sub-quota, of at least 7% of the quota for European works, for works created by independent producers and specifically aimed at minors.[404]

§3. Protection of Minors (Indecency and Violence)

200. In the framework of the rules designed to protect viewers' rights, a particular emphasis is placed on the safeguarding of the proper development of minors. Article 37 CLAVMS, in this connection, sets out a number of provisions governing the participation of minors in television shows, the content of programmes and

394. Article 53, para. 1, CLAVMS.
395. Article 53, para. 2(b), CLAVMS.
396. Article 53, para. 1, CLAVMS.
397. Article 53, para. 2(a), CLAVMS.
398. Article 53, para. 3, CLAVMS.
399. *Ibid.*
400. Article 54, para. 1, CLAVMS.
401. Article 54, para. 3, CLAVMS.
402. Article 54, para. 4, CLAVMS.
403. Article 54, para. 6, CLAVMS.
404. Article 54, para. 8, CLAVMS.

audiovisual commercial communications, etc.[405] Other relevant provisions are set out in the Self-Regulatory Code 'Media and Minors'.[406]

201. The CLAVMS sets out a general ban for programmes that may seriously impair the physical, mental, or moral development of minors (seriously harmful contents), such as those involving gratuitous violence or pornography, and for films forbidden to minors under the age of eighteen.[407]

202. By way of derogation, on-demand media service providers can transmit seriously harmful content,[408] provided that minors are prevented from normally viewing those programmes by way of suitable technical arrangements specified by AGCom by recourse to co-regulation procedures.[409] AGCom, to that end, set up a technical board open to all stakeholders[410] and, building upon the board's contributions, adopted a regulation concerning the technical arrangements that must be implemented to prevent minors from accessing audiovisual content that may seriously harm their development[411] as well as a regulation on the classification criteria for contents that may seriously harm the development of minors.[412]

203. Turning to linear media service providers, Article 37(2) CLAVMS prohibits the provision of audiovisual contents that may harm the physical, mental, or moral development of minors as well as films forbidden to minors under the age of fourteen (harmful contents). Those contents, however, can be provided without restrictions from 11 pm to 7 am or if technical arrangements are put in place so as to prevent minors from normally viewing the contents concerned.[413] In this case, the CLAVMS requires that an acoustic notice be transmitted prior to the beginning of those programmes and that they be constantly identified by means of a clearly perceivable visual notice. AGCom, via co-regulation procedures, may set out different and additional technical measures.[414]

204. The CLAVMS also requires media service providers to exercise particular care with reference to programmes and audiovisual commercial communications broadcast between 4 pm and 7 pm, that is, the period when most minors are presumed to be watching television.[415] Moreover, programme schedules must include

405. R. Zaccaria, A. Valastro, E. Albanesi, *Diritto dell'informazione e della comunicazione*, (Padua: Cedam, 2021); F. Bruno, G. Nava, *Il nuovo ordinamento delle comunicazioni. Radiotelevisione, comunicazionioni elettroniche, editoria* (Milano: Giuffrè, 2006), 828 et seq.
406. *See infra* n. 373.
407. Article 37, para. 1 CLAVMS.
408. Article 37, para. 3 CLAVMS.
409. Article 37, para. 5 CLAVMS.
410. AGCom, 224/12/CSP, 4 Oct. 2012. *See also* Francesca Pellicanò, AGCom Technical Board for the Protection of Minors in on Demand Services. IRIS 10 (2012): 18 et seq.
411. AGCom, 51/13/CSP, 3 May 2013.
412. AGCom, 52/13/CSP, 3 May 2013.
413. Article 37, para. 2 CLAVMS.
414. *Ibid.*
415. Article 37, para. 7 CLAVMS.

a certain number of programmes specifically targeted at a younger audience: that percentage is determined by AGCom in the framework of the European works transmission time quota.[416]

205. Finally, regard must be had to the Self-Regulatory Code 'Media and Minors', setting out a number of detailed provisions that flesh out the rules on the protection of minors laid down in the CLAVMS.[417] Albeit originally a self-regulatory instrument, the 'Media and Minors' Code has a legally binding nature by virtue of Article 37(6) CLAVMS, which required all media service providers to comply with the Code. Indeed, in case of infringement of the provisions of the 'Media and Minors' Code, its Supervision Committee can enjoin the media service provider concerned to comply with those provisions as well as to modify or discontinue the offending content. The Supervision Committee, moreover, may report the infringement to AGCom,[418] which can impose the sanctions laid down to that effect in the CLAVMS.[419]

206. The first part of the 'Media and Minors' Code sets out a number of general principles and goals, including a commitment to improve the quality of the programmes targeted to minors, to contribute to the education of the viewers, and to draw public attention to childhood issues.[420] The second part of the Code, instead, lays down a number of detailed duties for media service providers.

A first set of rules concerns participation by minors in television programmes, which can only occur so long as it does not jeopardize the minor's dignity.[421] Another group of provisions deals with the contents of the programme schedule, with a strong emphasis on the sensitive period between 4 pm and 7 pm, where media service providers are called upon to exercise great care for the interests of the minors in the choice of both programmes – which should include content expressly targeted at younger audiences – and advertising.[422]

As to the latter, the 'Media and Minors' Code lays down different protection levels: a *general* protection level, that applies at all times;[423] an *enhanced* protection level, that applies between 7 am and 4 pm as well as between 7 pm and 10:30 pm;[424] and a *specific* protection level, that applies between 4 pm and 7 pm, where particular care as to the recognizability of advertising must be exercised and where the advertising of alcoholic beverages, birth control means, and premium telephone services must be avoided.[425]

---

416. Article 37, para. 11 CLAVMS.
417. The full version of the Code is available at: http://www.agcom.it/default.aspx?message=visualizzadocument&DocID=3100.
418. Point (6) of Media and Minors Code.
419. Article 38, paras 2 and 3 CLAVMS.
420. Premise to the Media and Minors Code.
421. Point (1) of Media and Minors Code.
422. Point (3) of the Media and Minors Code.
423. Point (4.2) of the Media and Minors Code.
424. Point (4.3) of the Media and Minors Code.
425. Point (4.4) of the Media and Minors Code.

§4. Human Dignity and Other Fundamental Rights

207. The protection of human dignity is one of the overarching principles governing Italian AVMS legislation.[426] The CLAVMS contains several references to human dignity.

208. The protection of human dignity is one of the grounds that enables AGCom to restrict the reception or retransmission of media services at the request of other Member States.[427]

209. Human dignity must be respected in audiovisual commercial communications,[428] teleshopping,[429] as well as in the processing of personal data occurring in connection with the provision of media services.[430]

210. Media services supplied by service providers subject to Italian jurisdiction must not contain any incitement to commit any criminal offence, in particular, the incitement to violence or hatred[431] and to commit acts of terrorism.[432] AGCom must define, by means of a specific regulation, suitable binding criteria for media service providers so as to prevent the violation of these prohibitions.[433]

§5. Right of Reply

211. The CLAVMS expressly recognizes the right of reply in Article 35. Anyone who deems that his or her legitimate interests, in particular reputation and good name, have been damaged by an assertion of false facts in a television programme is entitled to request the relevant media service provider to broadcast a reply, provided that the content of that reply does not give rise to criminal responsibility.[434] The media service provider must transmit the reply within forty-eight hours from the request, at a time and in a manner appropriate and equivalent to those of the broadcast to which the request refers.

212. If the media service provider does not transmit the reply, the person concerned, without prejudice to ordinary judicial remedies, can forward his or her request to AGCom, which must adopt a decision within five days.[435] If AGCom

426. Article 4 CLAVMS.
427. Article 7, para. 12, letter (a), point (1) CLAVMS.
428. Article 43, para. 1, letter (c), point (1) CLAVMS.
429. Article 47, para. 1 CLAVMS.
430. Article 4, para. 5 CLAVMS.
431. Article 30, para. 1, letter (a) CLAVMS.
432. Article 30, para. 1, letter (b) CLAVMS.
433. Article 30, para. 2 CLAVMS.
434. Article 35, para. 2 CLAVMS.
435. Article 35, para. 4 CLAVMS.

upholds the request, the reply as well as a reference to AGCom's decision on the matter must be transmitted within twenty-four hours of said decision.[436]

213. Academic commentators have pointed out that the right of reply in the context of television broadcasting serves a different function than the right of reply under the Press Law. While the latter (as noted in Part II, Chapter 4, §2) seeks to safeguard individuals' dignity and personal identity[437] and indirectly the pluralism of information,[438] the right of reply under the CLAVMS is aimed at preserving the objectivity by restoring the truth, as the provision of an administrative remedy entrusted to AGCom suggests.[439]

§6. Accessibility to Users with Disabilities

214. The CLAVMS provides that media service providers shall develop action plans aimed at making their services more accessible to people with disabilities.[440]

215. AGCom shall take appropriate measures to ensure that media service providers accomplish that goal.[441] AGCom, having consulted the Ministry of Economic Development, shall also prepare a report for the European Commission to be transmitted by 19 December 2022 and subsequently, at least every three years.[442] Moreover, AGCom shall operate as a Single Online Point of Contact, available to the public and easily accessible to people with disabilities, in order to provide information and receive complaints.[443]

---

436. *Ibid.*
437. *See* A. Pace, M. Manetti, 'Art. 21: la libertà di manifestazione del proprio pensiero', *Commentario della Costituzione*, ed. G. Branca, A. Pizzorusso (Bologna: Zanichelli, 2006), 794.
438. *See* Court of Cassation, Judgment of 5 Apr. 1990, no. 2852. *See also* O. Grandinetti, *Il diritto di rettifica, Radiotelevisione*, ed. R. Zaccaria (Padua: Cedam, 1996), 569.
439. *See* A. Pace, M. Manetti, 'Art. 21: la libertà di manifestazione del proprio pensiero', *Commentario della Costituzione,* ed. G. Branca, A. Pizzorusso (Bologna: Zanichelli, 2006), 795.
440. Article 31, para. 2 CLAVMS.
441. Article 31, para. 1 CLAVMS.
442. Article 31, para. 3 CLAVMS.
443. Article 31, para. 6 CLAVMS.

Chapter 4. Political Broadcasting

§1. Rules on Political Independence of Media Providers

216. Before turning to the analysis of the rules devised by the legislature to ensure a level playing field in the access to political broadcasting, regard must be had to the logically antecedent issue of the de facto situation in Italy, characterized for several years, as the European Parliament put it, by 'a unique combination of economic, political and media power in the hands of one man', i.e., the former Prime Minister Silvio Berlusconi.[444]

217. Mr Berlusconi has been the largest shareholder of the Mediaset network group since its establishment in 1978 as well as the Prime Minister of Italy in office from 1994 to 1995, from 2001 to 2006 and from 2008 to 2011. According to scholarly commentators, this situation of conflict of interest may upset the balance of electoral competition, contrary to the constitutional principles of internal and external pluralism (Article 21), equality (Article 3), impartiality of public administration (Article 97), and equal access to public offices (Article 51).[445] Moreover, as duly noted by the European Parliament[446] and the Parliamentary Assembly of the Council of Europe,[447] this situation may impinge upon the principle of freedom of expression enshrined in Article 10 ECHR and in Article 11, paragraph 2, of the Charter of Fundamental Rights of the EU.

218. The debate on the conflict of interest sparked off in 1994, following Mr Berlusconi's first election and appointment as Prime Minister. Some Members of the Parliament claimed that Mr Berlusconi's election to the Chamber of Deputies was at variance with Article 10 of the Decree of the President of the Republic no. 361 of 1957, according to which holders of public concessions of a significant value cannot be elected to the Chamber of Deputies.[448] The Chamber's Committee of Elections, however, took the view that that provision only concerned persons

---

444. European Parliament, Resolution on the risks of violation, in the EU and especially in Italy, of freedom of expression and information (Art. 11(2) of the Charter of Fundamental Rights), 2003/2237(INI), para. 60.

445. *See* R. Zaccaria, A. Valastro, E. Albanesi, *Diritto dell'informazione e della comunicazione*, (Padua: Cedam, 2021).

446. *See*, for example, European Parliament, Resolution on the risks of violation, in the EU and especially in Italy, of freedom of expression and information (Art. 11(2) of the Charter of Fundamental Rights), 2003/2237(INI), para. 60; European Parliament, Resolution on the situation as regards fundamental rights in the EU (2002), 2002/2013(INI), para. 37 (deploring 'the fact that in Italy in particular a situation is continuing in which media power is concentrated in the hands of the Prime Minister, without any rules on conflict of interest having been adopted').

447. *See* Parliamentary Assembly of the Council of Europe, Resolution 1387 (2004), Monopolisation of the electronic media and possible abuse of power in Italy, para. 1 (expressing concern about 'concerned by the concentration of political, commercial and media power in the hands of one person, Prime Minister Silvio Berlusconi').

448. Decree of the President of the Republic 30 Mar. 1957, no. 361.

holding broadcasting concessions 'in their own name', not indirectly through shareholdings (as in the case of Mr Berlusconi).[449]

219. It was not until 2004 that the legislature passed a bill aimed at regulating the conflict of interest between public officials and professional and entrepreneurial activities, the so-called Frattini Law.[450]

The Frattini Law provides that holding a government office (e.g., the Prime Minister, ministers, etc.) is incompatible with the occupation of specific kinds of posts, such as those involving the management of business undertakings.[451] Individual entrepreneurs must entrust their undertakings to one or more trustees (including family members).[452]

The Frattini Law requires persons holding a government office to devote themselves exclusively to the public good and to abstain from taking measures and participating in joint decisions in situations where there is a conflict of interest.[453] Conflicts of interests are defined as an action or omission by persons holding a government office: (i) when they are also holding an incompatible post as defined above; or (ii) when that action or omission has a specific, preferential effect on the assets of the office-holder or of his or her spouse or relatives up to the second degree, or of companies or other undertakings controlled by them, to the detriment of the public interest.[454]

220. A number of academic commentators and institutional actors have expressed concerns as to the ability of the Frattini Law to effectively address the situation of conflict of interest characterizing the Italian media sector.[455] The Council of Europe Commission for Democracy through Law, in particular, highlighted a number of criticalities in the Frattini Law.[456] First, that law 'only declares a general incompatibility between the management of a company and public office, not between ownership as such and public office', albeit the latter appears to be the foremost aspect of the conflict of interest in Italy.[457] Second, by defining conflict of interest as including measures having 'a specific, preferential effect on the assets of the office-holder', the Frattini Law may be unable to prevent the office-holder

---

449. Chamber of Deputies, Committee for Elections, decisions of 20 Jul. 1994 and of 17 Oct. 1996.
450. Law 20 Jul. 2004, no. 215, 'Norme in materia di risoluzione dei conflitti di interessi'. The Frattini Law was named after its sponsor Minister Franco Frattini, at that time in charge of the Public Functions Department of the Berlusconi II Cabinet.
451. Article 2, para. 1, of the Frattini Law.
452. Article 2, para. 2, of the Frattini Law.
453. Article 1 of the Frattini Law.
454. Article 3 of the Frattini Law.
455. *See*, for example, B. Valensise, *Il conflitto di interessi nella legge n. 215 del 2004 tra luci (poche) ed ombre (molte)* (Studium iuris, 2005), 834 et seq. and 1034 et seq.; F. Scintola, *La disciplina del conflitto di interessi dei membri del Governo* (Nuova rassegna di legislazione, dottrina e giurisprudenza, 2005), 2131 et seq.; R. Zaccaria, A. Valastro, E. Albanesi, *Diritto dell'informazione e della comunicazione*, (Padua: Cedam, 2021).
456. European Commission for Democracy Through Law (Venice Commission), Opinion no. 309/ 2004 on the compatibility of the Laws 'Gasparri' and 'Frattini' of Italy with the Council of Europe standards in the field of freedom of expression and pluralism of the media, available at: www.venice.coe.int/ docs/2005/CDL-AD%282005%29017-e.asp#_ftn83.
457. *Ibid.*, para. 237.

abstaining 'from intervening in matters which generally and indirectly, though surely, affect his or her proprietary interests'.[458] Moreover, the need for such effect to be 'specific' and 'to the detriment of the public interest' implies a very high burden of proof, thus making the application of the Law extremely difficult in practice.[459]

§2. FAIR REPRESENTATION IN ELECTION PERIODS

221. The Constitutional Court has expressly recognized the right to fair representation in election periods.[460] According to academic commentators, that right stems from the constitutional principles of freedom of expression (Article 21), freedom of association (Article 49), equal access to public offices (Article 51), and popular sovereignty (Article 1, paragraph 2).[461]

222. Law no. 28 of 2000, as amended by Law no. 313 of 2003, seeks to ensure a level playing field for all political actors during the electoral period.[462] That law applies to three categories of programmes: political communication programmes, information programmes, and self-managed slots (*messaggi autogestiti*).

Political communication programmes include all programmes entailing a political opinion or assessment, but not the diffusion of news in information programmes. Information programmes account for the most significant part of the political debate on television; the Constitutional Court clarified that this category also includes the presentation of news in a narrative or argumentative context.[463] Self-managed slots are time periods of a predetermined duration assigned to a plurality of political actors where the latter can inform the public about their platform or programme.

223. Those three categories of programmes are subject to a number of general requirements (which will be examined in §§ 3 and 4 below), plus some specific rules during electoral periods. If broadcasters infringe those rules, AGCom can impose sanctions either by its own motion or following a request by the political actor concerned. Those sanctions may seek to restore the balance by granting the harmed party additional time in the course of political communication programmes or additional self-managed slots. In case of serious violations, AGCom may enjoin the broadcaster concerned to give notice of the infringement decision and, if necessary, to air a reply by the harmed party, which must be given the same visibility (in terms of time slot, presentation, etc.) of the offending broadcast. Broadcasters may challenge the above decisions before administrative courts.[464]

---

458. *Ibid.*, para. 236.
459. *Ibid.*, para. 240.
460. *See*, for example, Constitutional Court Judgment nos 48/1964, 161/1995, 155/2002.
461. *See* R. Zaccaria, A. Valastro, E. Albanesi, *Diritto dell'informazione e della comunicazione*, (Padua: Cedam, 2021).
462. Article 1 of Law 28 of 2000.
463. Constitutional Court, Judgment no. 155/2002.
464. Article 10 of Law no. 28 of 2000.

224. Political communication in electoral periods can only take place in the form of political forums, debates, round tables, adversarial presentations of candidates and political programmes, interviews and any other form that allows the comparison between the political positions and candidates.[465]

Self-managed slots during electoral periods are subject to stringent rules as to their remuneration and allotment to political actors.[466]

225. Turning to information programmes, for each electoral campaign the PSC and AGCom adopt ad hoc regulations laying down detailed rules for those programmes during the electoral period.[467] AGCom also establishes a *par condicio* task force to monitor compliance with those rules.

226. On the days of the elections, it is forbidden for all television broadcasts to provide, either directly or indirectly, voting suggestions or to express voting preferences.[468]

Programme presenters and anchorpersons are required to behave in a fair and impartial manner so as not to exert a disguised influence on the audience's freedom of vote.[469]

Moreover, in the fifteen days preceding the elections, it is forbidden to publish or otherwise disseminate the results of opinion polls on the outcome of elections and the political orientations of voters, even if such surveys were prepared at an earlier date.[470]

§3. News and Current Affairs Programmes

227. Article 6 CLAVMS provides that information programmes must be, *inter alia*, truthful and open to all political actors. Paragraph 3 thereof entrusts AGCom with the task of laying down detailed rules implementing the principles set out in the CLARMS. Accordingly, AGCom adopted Decision no. 22/06/CSP setting out

465. Article 4, para. 1, of Law no. 28 of 2000.
466. Article 4 of Law no. 28 of 2000.
467. *See*, for example, AGCom Decision no. 153/11/CSP, 'Disposizioni di attuazione della disciplina in materia di comunicazione politica e di parità di accesso ai mezzi di informazione relative alla campagna per i referendum consultivi indetti dal Comune di Milano per i giorni 12 e 13 giugno 2011'; no. 151/11/CSP, Ordine conformativo alla Rai-Radiotelevisione Italiana Spa per l'effettivo rispetto della deliberazione della Commissione parlamentare per l'indirizzo generale e la vigilanza sui servizi radiotelevisivi recante 'Disposizioni in materia di comunicazione politica, messaggi autogestiti e informazione della concessionaria pubblica nonché tribune relative alla campagna per i referendum popolari indetti per i giorni 12 e 13 giugno 2011'; no. 152/11/CSP, 'Invito alle emittenti televisive nazionali private ad assicurare l'informazione sui referendum popolari indetti per i giorni del 12 e 13 giugno 2011'.
468. Article 5, para. 2, of Law no. 28 of 2000.
469. Article 5, para. 3, of Law no. 28 of 2000.
470. Article 8, para. 1, of Law no. 28 of 2000.

implementing provisions on equal access to information programmes in non-electoral periods.[471]

228. All information programmes, including news broadcasts and in-depth factual programming, must comply with the principles of comprehensiveness and accuracy of information, objectivity, fairness, honesty, impartiality, pluralism, and equal treatment.[472]

229. A balance in the attendance of political actors must be ensured throughout the schedule of a given information programme, if possible by publishing such schedule in advance.[473] The Latium Regional Administrative Court clarified that, in non-electoral periods, such a balance must be understood in qualitative terms (i.e., the attitude towards certain political actors or topics) rather than in quantitative terms (i.e., the number of guests from a certain political faction or their talking time).[474] Quantitative analysis, instead, must be applied in pre-electoral periods: should the political balance be upset in favour of a political faction, it must be restored on the next available occasion.[475]

230. Programme presenters must run their programmes in a fair and impartial manner – also as far as the selection and involvement of studio audience are concerned – so as not to affect the process of forming political opinions. The provision of information must be kept quite distinct from its comment and critique.[476]

231. Entertainment programmes, as a rule, should not host political actors, unless those programmes deal with topics on which political actors have a specific competence or expertise.[477] In that case, the relevant parts will be regarded as an 'informative window' within an entertainment programme. Such informative windows are subject to the same rules applying to information programmes.

§4. Political Advertising

232. While news and current affairs programmes must represent a plurality of political views, political advertising is designed to allow political actors to unilaterally inform the audience about their political platform or agenda. Political advertising in the form of self-managed slots (*messaggi autogestiti*) is governed by

471. AGCom Decision no. 22/06/CSP, 'Disposizioni applicative delle norme e dei principi vigenti in materia di comunicazione politica e parità di accesso ai mezzi di informazione nei periodi non elettorali'.
472. Article 2, para. 1, of Decision no. 22/06/CSP. *See also* O. Grandinetti, *Par condicio e programmi di informazione*, Giornale di diritto amministrativo (2008): 1157 et seq.
473. Article 2, para. 2, of Decision no. 22/06/CSP.
474. Latium Regional Administrative Court, judgment no. 1392/2014 and 1394/2014.
475. Article 2, para. 3, of Decision no. 22/06/CSP.
476. Article 2, para. 6, of Decision no. 22/06/CSP.
477. Article 3, para. 2, of Decision no. 22/06/CSP.

Article 3 of Law no. 28 of 2000 and AGCom Decision no. 200/00/CSP.[478] Broadcasting self-managed slots is compulsory for the PSM operator and optional for commercial broadcasters.[479]

233. Self-managed slots, which usually last between one and three minutes, are not inserted during programmes but are broadcast in the context of specific container programmes.[480] The amount of self-managed slots cannot exceed 25% of the total transmission time devoted to political communication programmes by each broadcaster or by each network within the same week and within the same time periods.[481] No more than two container programmes can be broadcasted daily.[482] Self-managed slots are not taken into account for the purpose of advertising limits.

234. Self-managed slots are allotted to political actors under non-discriminatory terms. Slots within each container programme are allocated through a draw. No political actor can be assigned more than two slots within the same container programme. Each slot must clearly identify the political actor to which it has been allotted.[483]

---

478. AGCom Decision no. 200/00/CSP, 'Disposizioni di attuazione della disciplina in materia di comunicazione politica e di parità di accesso ai mezzi di informazione nei periodi non elettorali'.
479. Article 3, para. 2, of Law no. 28 of 2000.
480. Article 3, para. 3, of Law no. 28 of 2000.
481. Article 3, para. 4, of Law no. 28 of 2000.
482. *Ibid.*
483. Article 3, para. 6, of Law no. 28 of 2000.

Chapter 5. Advertising Rules

§1. Various Forms of Commercial Communications

235. The CLAVMS defines audiovisual commercial communications as images with or without sound, which are designed to promote, directly or indirectly, the goods, services or image of a natural or legal entity pursuing an economic activity.[484] Such images accompany or are included in a programme or in user-generated content in return for payment or similar consideration or for self-promotional purposes.[485]

236. The notion of audiovisual commercial communications includes the following: (i) television advertising; (ii) teleshopping; (iii) sponsorship; (iv) telepromotions; and (iv) product placement.[486]

I. Television Advertising and Self-promotion

237. According to the CLAVMS, 'television advertising' is a form of audiovisual commercial communication taking the form of an announcement broadcast, whether in return for payment or for similar consideration or for self-promotional purposes, by a public or private undertaking or a natural person in connection with a trade, business, craft or profession in order to promote, in return for payment, the supply of goods or services, including immovable property, rights and obligations.[487]

238. 'Advertising spots' are a type of advertising having predetermined content broadcast by digital or analogue television broadcasters.[488] In this connection, it must be noted that the notion of advertising spots employed in the CLAVMS does not reflect the criteria set out in Recital no. 87 AVMSD, according to which advertising spots should be understood as television advertising having a duration of not more than twelve minutes.[489]

239. 'Telepromotion' is a form of television advertising consisting of the verbal and visual presentation of products or services, produced by the audiovisual media service provider or the broadcaster, in the course of a programme with a view to promoting, in return for payment, those products or services.[490] Telepromotion, in other words, is based on the interruption of studio programmes (especially game

484. Article 3, para. 1, letter (oo) CLAVMS.
485. *Ibid.*
486. *Ibid.*
487. Article 3, para. 1, letter (pp) CLAVMS.
488. Article 3, para. 1, letter (qq) CLAVMS.
489. *See* R. Mastroianni, A. Arena, 'Italy: Draft Decree Implementing the Audiovisual Media Services Directive'. IRIS, 2 (2010): 25 et seq., available at: http://merlin.obs.coe.int/iris/2010/2/article25.en.html.
490. *See* Art. 3, para. 1, letter (vv) CLAVMS.

shows) by slots devoted to the presentation of one or more products or services, where the programme presenters momentarily swap their role for one as 'promoters' of the goods or services concerned.[491]

240. 'Split-screen advertising' consists of the simultaneous or parallel transmission of editorial content and advertising content. For example, one or more advertising spots appear in a window during the transmission of a programme in such a way that two separate images are visible on the screen. Provided the space set aside for advertising is not excessive, this technique enables the viewer to continue to watch the editorial programme during the transmission of an advertising spot.[492]

241. Self-promotion consists of announcements made by broadcasters and audiovisual media service providers in relation to their own programmes or directly derived collateral products or in relation to programs and AVMS of other entities that are part of the same corporate group.[493] The consistency with the AVMSD of the extension of the notion of self-promotion to announcements made by broadcasters to radio programs of entities that are part of the same corporate group is currently being assessed by the ECJ.[494]

The legal classification of self-promotion has proven problematic. On the one hand, CLAVMS appears to classify self-promotion as a type of television advertising by stating that, in Article 3(1)(pp), television advertising can take place either in return for payment or 'for self-promotional purposes'.[495] On the other hand, Article 45(5) CLAVMS stipulates that the time devoted by a media service provider to promote its own programmes or collateral products must not be taken into account for the purpose of daily and hourly advertising limits.

II. Teleshopping

242. 'Teleshopping' is a type of audiovisual commercial communication distinct from television advertising. Teleshopping consists of direct offers broadcast to the public with a view to the supply of goods or services, including immovable property, rights and obligations, in return for payment.[496]

243. The CLAVMS refers to two subcategories of teleshopping: teleshopping windows and teleshopping spots.[497] Teleshopping spots are not defined in CLAVMS but are subject to the same rules applying to advertising spots.[498]

---

491. *See* Commission interpretative communication on certain aspects of the provisions on televised advertising in the 'Television without frontiers' Directive (2004/C 102/02), para. 25.
492. *Ibid.*, para. 41.
493. Article 3, para. 1, letter (eee) CLAVMS.
494. Pending Case C-255/21, *Reti televisive italiane.*
495. Article 3, para. 1, letter (pp) CLAVMS.
496. Article 3, para. 1, letter (tt) CLAVMS.
497. *See* A. Arena, 'Rules Governing Teleshopping Amended'. IRIS 5 (2008): 24 et seq., available at: http://merlin.obs.coe.int/iris/2008/5/article24.en.html.
498. *See*, for example, Article 44, para. 2, CLAVMS.

244. Teleshopping windows are programmes consisting exclusively of offers to the public; they must be kept quite distinct from other programmes by optical or acoustic means and must have a minimum uninterrupted duration of fifteen minutes.[499]

III. Sponsorship

245. Sponsorship can be defined as a contribution made by public or private undertakings or natural persons not engaged in the provision of media services, video-sharing platform services, or the production of audiovisual works, to the financing of media services, video-sharing platform services, user-generated videos, or programmes with a view to promoting their name, trade mark, image, activities, or products.[500]

IV. Product Placement

246. Product placement is a form of audiovisual commercial communication consisting in the inclusion of or reference to a product, a service or the trademark thereof so that it is featured in a programme or a user-generated video, in return for payment or other consideration.[501]

§2. Restrictions on Content

247. Article 43 CLAVMS, implementing Article 9 AVMSD, lays down a number of requirements applying to all types of audiovisual commercial communications. It is worth reminding that those restrictions also apply to radio broadcasters and the providers of video-sharing platform providers.[502]

248. Audiovisual commercial communications must not prejudice respect for human dignity, include or promote discrimination of any sort, or encourage behaviour prejudicial to health, safety, or the protection of the environment.[503]

249. Special restrictions apply to audiovisual commercial communications concerning certain products: cigarettes and tobacco products, including electronic cigarettes and refill containers, cannot be the subject of any type of audiovisual commercial communications, even in indirect form (i.e., through the promotion of names, trademarks, logos, or other features of tobacco products or brand);[504] the same ban applies to medicinal products and medical treatment available only on

499. Article 47, para. 3, CLAVMS.
500. Article 3, para. 1, letter (ss) CLAVMS.
501. Article 3, para. 1, letter (uu) CLAVMS.
502. Article 43, para. 5 CLAVMS.
503. Article 43, para. 1, letter (c) CLAVMS.
504. Article 43, para. 1, letter (d) CLAVMS.

prescription;[505] audiovisual commercial communications for alcoholic beverages must not be aimed specifically at minors or encourage immoderate consumption of such beverages.[506]

250. Turning to the protection of minors, the CLAVMS provides that audiovisual commercial communications must not cause physical or moral harm to them. Thus, audiovisual commercial communications must not directly exhort minors to purchase a product or service by exploiting their inexperience or credulity, directly encourage them to persuade their parents or others to purchase the goods or services being advertised, exploit the special trust minors place in parents, teachers or other persons, or unreasonably show minors in dangerous situations.[507]

The CLAVMS encourages media service providers to develop codes of conduct regarding inappropriate audiovisual commercial communications related to alcoholic beverages and accompanying or included in children's programmes concerning foods and beverages, including supplements, containing nutrients and substances with a nutritional or physiological effect, excessive intakes of which in the overall diet are not recommended.[508]

251. The rules on advertising contents set out in the CLAVMS are fleshed out by a number of self-regulation and co-regulation instruments, such as the Self-Regulation Code 'Media and Minors',[509] the Advertising Self-Regulation Code,[510] etc.

§3. Time and Frequency Restrictions

I. Time Restrictions (Advertising Limits)

252. Advertising limits define the quantity of television advertising and teleshopping spots that can be broadcast over a specified period of time. Self-promotion by a broadcaster of its own programmes, sponsorship notices, product placement, as well as neutral frames between editorial content and television advertising or teleshopping spots, and between individual spots are not taken into account for the purpose of advertising limits.[511] The same holds true, subject to certain requirements, for promotional messages transmitted free of charge or on favourable terms intended to promote books and upcoming European cinematographic works.[512]

505. Article 43, para. 1, letter (f) CLAVMS.
506. Article 43, para. 1, letter (e) CLAVMS. *See also* the specific provisions for on-demand providers laid down Article 43, para. 3, CLAVMS and those on the television advertising and teleshopping of alcoholic beverages laid down in Art. 44, para. 9 CLAVMS.
507. Article 43, para. 1, letter (g) CLAVMS.
508. Article 43, para. 4 CLAVMS.
509. *See*, in particular, s. 4 of the 'Media and Minors' Code (*see* n. 313).
510. The latest version of the Code is available at: www.iap.it/it/codice.htm.
511. Article 45, para. 5 CLAVMS.
512. Article 45, para. 10 CLAVMS.

253. The CLAVMS envisages different advertising limits for different categories of audiovisual media service providers, which will be examined seriatim. Contract clauses requiring broadcasters to schedule advertising beyond those limits are null and void.[513] Failure by audiovisual media service providers to comply with advertising limits may result in the imposition of fines by AGCom.

254. The PSM operator can schedule advertising of any form for up to 7% (6% as of 1 January 2023) of the airtime between 6 am and 6 pm and of the airtime between 6 pm and 12 am. In addition, the PSM operator is subject to an hourly limit: it can schedule advertising for up to 12% of every hour of airtime.[514]

255. Turning to other audiovisual media service providers, nationwide free-to-air media providers can schedule advertising spots, telepromotions, and teleshopping for up to 20% of the airtime between 6 am and 6 pm and of the airtime between 6 pm and 12 am.[515] Pay-TV media providers can schedule advertising spots, telepromotions, and teleshopping for up to 15% of the airtime between 6 am and 6 pm and of the airtime between 6 pm and 12 am.[516]

256. The compatibility with EU law and the Italian Constitution of the provision of different advertising limits for Pay-TV and free-to-air providers was the subject of a lawsuit involving both the ECJ and the Constitutional Court. The ECJ ruled in 2013 that granting Pay-TV users a stronger level of protection against excess advertising is in line with EU law, as long as such differential treatment is proportionate to the aim pursued.[517] In its judgment No. 210/2015, the Constitutional Court ruled that enabling free-to-air providers to broadcast more advertising than Pay-TV providers was consistent with the Italian Constitution.[518]

257. Finally, local television broadcasters, including analogue broadcasters, can transmit advertising for up to 25% limit of the airtime between 6 am and 6 pm and of the airtime between 6 pm and 12 am.[519]

II. Frequency Restrictions of Advertising Breaks

258. Article 44 CLAVMS sets out a number of provisions governing the insertion of teleshopping and advertising breaks during television broadcasts. Those rules apply *mutatis mutandis* to radio broadcasting.[520]

---

513. Article 45, para. 9 CLAVMS.
514. Article 45, para. 1 CLAVMS.
515. Article 45, para. 3 CLAVMS.
516. Article 45, para. 4 CLAVMS.
517. Judgment of the Court of 18 Jul. 2013, *Sky Italia Srl v. Autorità per le Garanzie nelle Comunicazioni*, Case C-234/12. *See also* Arena A, Rules on Italy's Stricter Hourly Advertising Limits for Pay-Tv Broadcasters, IRIS 8 (2013): 7 et seq., available at: http://merlin.obs.coe.int/iris/2013/8/article7.en.html.
518. Constitutional Court, Judgment no. 210 of 2015.
519. Article 45, para. 8, CLAVMS.
520. Article 44, para. 11 CLAVMS.

259. Television advertising and teleshopping must be readily recognizable as such and must be kept quite distinct from other parts of the programme by way of optical or acoustic means, as well as spatial means.[521] Accordingly, AGCom clarified that new advertising techniques such as split-screen and in-spots are allowed.[522] Moreover, the sound level of television advertising and teleshopping shall not exceed the ordinary level of the programmes and shall comply with the limits established by AGCom.[523]

260. CLAVMS further provides that isolated advertising and teleshopping spots must remain an exception, in order to minimize their impact on the integrity of programmes.[524] Nevertheless, CLAVMS does not specify a benchmark as to how to quantify such an exception: arguably, reference should be had to the percentage of isolated spots broadcasted within each programme.[525] Instead, the insertion of the so-called minispots during football matches and other sports programmes, which had given rise to a lively academic debate, is expressly allowed under Article 44, paragraph 2, CLAVMS.

261. Teleshopping and advertising spots can be inserted during a programme, provided that the latter's integrity is not unreasonably affected: the CLAVMS, in this regard provides, that regard must be had to a programme's natural breaks, to its duration and nature, as well as to the rights of the right holders.[526] In the case of sports events, the notion of 'natural break' must be determined in accordance with the relevant laws of the game (e.g., in the case of soccer, regard must be had to the fifteen-minute half-time break between halves).[527]

262. As far as the insertion of teleshopping and advertising spots during programmes is concerned, the CLAVMS sets out specific provisions for each of the main categories of television programmes: (i) news, films made for television (excluding series, serials, and documentaries), cinematographic works and news programmes can be interrupted by advertising and teleshopping spots no more than once for each scheduled period of at least thirty minutes;[528] (ii) children's programmes may be interrupted once for each scheduled period of at least thirty minutes, provided that the scheduled duration of the programme is greater than thirty minutes (the interruption of children's programmes is always prohibited in case of advertising spots or teleshopping relating to gambling);[529] (iii) no television advertising or teleshopping spots can be inserted during religious services;[530] (iv) the

---

521. Article 44, para. 1 CLAVMS.
522. *See* Art. 5 of AGCom Interpretative communication on television advertising.
523. Article 44, para. 1 CLAVMS.
524. Article 44, para. 2 CLAVMS.
525. *See* R. Mastroianni, *La direttiva sui servizi di media audiovisivi*, 116–117.
526. Article 44, para. 2 CLAVMS.
527. Latium Regional Administrative Court, Order of 23 Nov. 2005, complaint no. 13434/2001.
528. Article 44, para. 4 CLAVMS.
529. Article 44, para. 5 CLAVMS.
530. *Ibid.*

insertion of advertising and teleshopping spots during drama, opera and musicals is allowed insofar as it respects the breaks normally taking place when those works are displayed in theatres.[531]

263. The CLAVMS also sets out specific rules on advertising breaks for local media providers whose programmes are intended solely for the national territory and which cannot be received directly or indirectly by the public in one or more other Member States.[532] With reference to drama, opera, musicals and cinematographic works, local media providers can schedule, in addition to the advertising breaks displayed during the natural breaks of the programme, two additional advertising breaks for each act (or part) of the work, regardless of the latter's duration.[533] For works lasting 110 minutes or more, local broadcasters can schedule three advertising breaks plus an additional break for every period of thirty minutes exceeding the 110-minute threshold.[534]

264. Moreover, the CLAVMS defines the notion of 'scheduled duration' of a programme: that is the transmission time between the beginning of the opening theme and the end of the closing theme of a programme, including advertising breaks scheduled in between, as per the programme schedule.[535]

§4. Sponsorship

265. According to the CLAVMS, AVMS or programmes that are sponsored must comply with a number of requirements: (i) their content and, in the case of television broadcasting, their scheduling must not be influenced in such a way as to affect the responsibility and editorial independence of the media service provider;[536] (ii) they must be clearly identified as such by the name or logo or any other distinctive symbol or sign of the sponsor at the beginning and at the end of the programmes;[537] (iii) they must not directly encourage the purchase or rental of goods or services, in particular by making specific promotional references to those goods or services.[538]

266. The CLAVMS also lays down some restrictions as to the type of businesses allowed to engage in sponsorship: (i) firms whose principal activity is the manufacture or sale of cigarettes, electronic cigarettes, refill containers, or other tobacco or nicotine products cannot sponsor AVMS or programmes;[539] (ii) firms whose activities include the manufacture or sale of medicinal products and medical

531. Article 44, para. 3 CLAVMS.
532. Article 26 AVMSD provides explicitly for this possibility.
533. Article 44, para. 6, CLAVMS.
534. *Ibid.*
535. Article 44, para. 7 CLAVMS.
536. Article 46, para. 1, letter (a) CLAVMS.
537. Article 46, para. 1, letter (b) CLAVMS.
538. Article 46, para. 1, letter (c) CLAVMS.
539. Article 46, para. 2, CLAVMS.

treatments, instead, may promote the name or the image of the firm through sponsorships, but cannot promote specific medicinal products, medical devices referred to in Regulation (EU) No 2017/745 or medical treatments available only on prescription.[540]

267. Moreover, some categories of programmes cannot be sponsored. This is the case with news and political affairs programmes.[541] The CLAVMS also prohibits showing sponsorship logos during children's programmes, documentaries, and religious programmes.[542]

§5. Product Placement

268. Pursuant to Article 48 CLAVMS, product placement in programs produced prior to 19 December 2009 is allowed in cinematographic works, films and series made for AVMS, sports programmes and light entertainment programmes.[543] In programs produced after 19 December 2009, product placement is permitted in all types of AVMS, except for news and current affairs programs, consumer programs, religious programs, and children's programs.[544]

269. The CLAVMS states that viewers must be clearly informed of product placement through appropriate means at the beginning and at the end of the programme and when the programme resumes after an advertising break, in order to avoid any possible confusion on the part of the viewer.[545]

270. The CLAVMS also provides that the content of programmes including product placement as well as their place in the programme schedule (in the case of linear media services) or catalogue (in the case of non-linear media services) must not be influenced in such a way as to affect the responsibility and editorial independence of the media service provider.[546]

271. Programmes containing product placement, moreover, must neither directly encourage the purchase or rental of goods or services (in particular by making special promotional references to those goods or services), nor give undue prominence to the product in question.[547]

272. Moreover, the CLAVMS expressly prohibits programmes containing product placement of cigarettes and other tobacco products or products containing nicotine, as well as electronic cigarettes and containers of refill liquid (or product

540. Article 46, para. 3, CLAVMS.
541. Article 46, para. 5, CLAVMS.
542. Article 46, para. 6 CLAVMS.
543. Article 48, para. 1 CLAVMS.
544. Article 48, para. 2, CLAVMS.
545. Article 48, para. 3, letter (d), CLAVMS.
546. Article 48, para. 3, letter (a) CLAVMS.
547. Article 48, para. 3, letters (b) and (c) CLAVMS.

placement from undertakings whose principal activity is the manufacture or sale of those products) as well as of specific medicines, medical devices referred to in Regulation (EU) No. 2017/745 or medical treatment that can be obtained exclusively on prescription within the Italian territory.[548]

273. The CLAVMS entrusts the implementation of the criteria above to self-regulation processes involving producers, broadcasters, advertising agencies, and other stakeholders.[549] In 2010, AGCom adopted a notice defining the scope and basic principles of self-regulation in the area of product placement and noted that the adoption of those self-regulation instruments is a necessary precondition if broadcasters intend to engage in product placement.[550] In 2011, AGCom established a Permanent Observatory on Product Placement to promote the adoption of those self-regulation instruments.[551]

548. Article 48, para. 4, letters (a) and (b) CLAVMS.
549. Article 48, para. 5 CLAVMS.
550. AGCom, notice of 25 Oct. 2010 concerning product placamento self-regulation, available at: www.agcom.it/default.aspx?DocID=5102.
551. AGCom Decision no. 19/11/CSP.

Chapter 6. Right to Information

274. The right to receive information is, as noted in Part I, one of the facets of the freedom of expression enshrined in Article 21 of the Italian Constitution. In the field of AVMS, this right is fleshed out by a number of provisions of the CLAVMS.[552]

275. Article 6(1) CLAVMS states that the provision of information through audiovisual media and radio services is a service of general interest. Accordingly, national and local media service providers are required, *inter alia*, to broadcast news programmes on a daily basis.[553] The Constitutional Court in 1998 dismissed the constitutionality question of an analogous requirement set out in the Mammì Law, thus suggesting that even the programming requirement laid down in the CLAVMS is compatible with the constitutional principles of equality (Article 1), freedom of expression (Article 21) and freedom of enterprise (Article 41).[554]

276. Another means devised by the Italian legislature to ensure the right to be informed is the requirement imposed on all media service providers subject to the Italian jurisdiction to provide the viewers with easy, direct, and permanent access to the following information: (i) the name of the media service provider; (ii) the address of its registered office; (iii) its contact information, including website and e-mail address; (iv) contact information for the departments of AGCom and of the Italian Antitrust Authority dealing with users' rights.[555]

§1. Access to Major Events

277. Under the AVMSD, 'major events' are events that each Member State regards as being of major importance for society and that accordingly must be accessible on free television to the public in that Member State.[556] The CLAVMS entrusts the Ministry of Economic Development, after consulting AGCom, with the task of drawing up Italy's list of major events and determining whether those events should be made available live or in deferred coverage, in whole or in part.[557]

278. That list is then transmitted to the Commission, which must verify its compatibility with EU law and forward it to the other Member States.[558] The other Member States must ensure that media service providers under their jurisdiction do

552. *See* generally P. Costanzo, G. De Minico, R. Zaccaria (eds), *I 'tre codici' della società dell'informazione: amministrazione digitale, comunicazioni elettroniche e contenuti audiovisivi* (Turin: Giappichelli, 2006); F. Donati, *L'ordinamento amministrativo delle comunicazioni* (Turin: Giappichelli, 2007).
553. Article 6, para. 2(b) CLAVMS.
554. *See* Constitutional Court, Order no. 38 of 1998.
555. Article 29, para. 3, CLAVMS.
556. Article 14, para. 1, AVMSD.
557. Article 33, para. 1, CLAVMS.
558. Article 14, para. 2, AVMSD.

not exercise exclusive rights in such a way that a substantial proportion of the Italian public is deprived of the possibility of following the major events on Italy's list.[559] Likewise, Italy must ensure, by appropriate means, that media service providers under its jurisdiction do not deprive a substantial proportion of the public of other Member States of the possibility of following major events on those Member States' lists.[560] To this end, AGCom adopts a resolution that identifies such 'appropriate means'.[561]

279. AGCom Decision no. 8/99/CONS[562] provides that 'events of major importance for society' are sport or non-sport events which meet at least two of the following criteria: (i) the event must be of general resonance in Italy also for people that do not usually follow that type of events; (ii) the event is widely recognized by the population, has particular cultural relevance, and is a catalyst of Italian cultural identity; (iii) the event involves the Italian national team in the context of a major international tournament; (iv) the event has been traditionally broadcast on free-to-air television and been followed by a substantial number of viewers in Italy.

280. AGCom Decision no. 172/99/CONS[563] included the following list of major events: (a) the summer and winter Olympics; (b) the finals and all the matches of the Fédération Internationale de Football Association (FIFA) World Cup involving the Italian national football team; (c) the finals and all the matches of the Union of European Football Associations (UEFA) European Football Championship involving the Italian national football team; (d) all the matches, home and away, involving the Italian national football team in the context of official competitions; (e) the finals and semi-finals involving Italian football clubs of the UEFA Champions League and of the UEFA Europa League; (f) the *Giro d'Italia*; (g) the Italian Grand Prix; (h) the Sanremo Music Festival.

281. In 2010 AGCom launched a public consultation on the amendment of the Italian list of major events.[564] The list currently in force was approved by AGCom Decision no. 131/12/CONS and includes the following events: (a) the Summer and Winter Olympics; (b) the final and all matches of the Italian national football team in the World Football Championship; (c) the final and all matches of the Italian national football team in the European Football Championship; (d) all matches played by the Italian national football team, at home and away, in official competitions; (e) the final and the semi-finals of the Champions League and the Europa League if Italian teams are involved; (f) the *Giro d'Italia*; (g) the Formula 1 Italian Grand Prix; (h) the Moto GP Italian Grand Prix; (i) the finals and semi-finals of the world championships in basketball, water polo, volleyball and rugby in which the Italian national team participates; (l) the matches of the Six Nations rugby tournament in which the Italian national team participates; (m) the finals and semi-finals

559. Article 14, para. 3, AVMSD.
560. *Ibid.*
561. Article 33, para. 2, CLAVMS.
562. AGCom Decision no. 8/99/CONS as amended by Decision no. 172/ 99/CONS.
563. Decision no. 172/99/CONS.
564. AGCom Decision no. 302/10/CONS.

of the Davis Cup and the Fed Cup in which the Italian national team participates and the 'Internazionali d'Italia' tennis tournament in which Italian athletes participate; (n) the World Road Cycling Championships; (o) the Sanremo Italian Music Festival; (p) the first performance of the opera season of the La Scala Theatre in Milan and of the San Carlo Theatre in Naples; (q) the New Year's Concert at La Fenice Theatre in Venice.[565]

282. Article 33 CLAVMS also entrusts the Ministry of Economic Development, after having heard AGCom, with the task of identifying the events of social interest or great public interest, the fruition of which must be guaranteed in compliance with adequate standards of regularity, continuity of service, and image quality.[566] Those standards are set up by AGCom in agreement with the Ministry of Economic Development.[567] AGCom also monitors the implementation of the above-mentioned provisions.[568]

§2. Short News Reporting

283. Article 15 AVMSD requires Member States to ensure that any broadcaster established in the EU has access on a fair, reasonable and non-discriminatory basis to events of high interest to the public, which are transmitted on an exclusive basis by a broadcaster under their jurisdiction for the purpose of short news reports. Article 34 CLAVMS entrusted AGCom with the task of regulating access for the purposes of short news reports to events of high public interest transmitted on an exclusive basis by Italian broadcasters. AGCom carried out that task by adopting the Short News Reports Regulation attached to AGCom Decision no. 667/10/CONS[569] as amended by Decision no. 392/12/CONS.[570]

284. The Short News Reports Regulation provides a definition of 'events of high public interest' and a non-exhaustive list of such events.[571] That list includes all the events mentioned in the draft list of major events attached to AGCom Decision no. 302/10/CONS (*see* §1 above), plus the four Grand Slam tennis tournaments, events of cultural or artistic value (such as festivals, fairs, and contests), religious events, and events of significant public interest.

285. All broadcasters are entitled to access high public interest events for the purpose of short news reports.[572] That right is qualified for local broadcasters, which are only granted access to events that may be of interest to their local audience.[573]

565. Annex B to the Decision no. 131/2012/CONS.
566. Article 33, para. 3, CLAVMS.
567. Article 33, para. 4, CLAVMS.
568. Article 33, para. 5, CLAVMS.
569. Attachment A to AGCom Decision no. 667/10/CONS.
570. Decision no. 392/12/CONS.
571. *Ibid.*, Art. 1, para. 1, letter (c).
572. *Ibid.*, Art. 3, para. 1.
573. *Ibid.*, Art. 3, para. 2.

On-demand service providers, in turn, may show short news reports only as parts of identical programmes already shown by a linear audiovisual media service provider.[574]

286. According to AGCom Decision no. 667/10/CONS, access to events of high public interest was originally allowed for up to three minutes for each event and only for the purposes of news reports shown from one to forty-eight hours after the end of the relevant event.[575] However, the Latium Regional Administrative Court and, on appeal, the Council of State ruled that that provision was at variance with Recital no. 55 of the AVMSD, according to which short news reports 'should not exceed ninety seconds'.[576] AGCom, accordingly, amended its decision so as to bring it in line with the AVMS Directive.[577] In the case of events having a very short duration, short news reports must have a maximum duration of no more than 3% of the overall duration of the event.[578] That provision is without prejudice to the ninety-second limit imposed by the AVMS Directive.[579]

287. As a rule, the organizer of a high public interest event should directly grant broadcasters access to the whole event, so that broadcasters can freely choose short extracts of the duration specified above.[580]

Failing that, broadcasters are entitled to access the signal of the broadcaster that has acquired exclusive rights to the event to freely choose short extracts of a maximum duration of three minutes. In that case, the broadcasters concerned must clearly identify their source throughout the extract.[581]

Access to high public interest events must be provided on fair, reasonable and non-discriminatory terms and at cost-oriented prices.[582]

288. Disputes between broadcasters concerning the classification of a given event as an event of high public interest, access terms and prices are subject to a settlement procedure before AGCom.[583]

574. *Ibid.*, Art. 3, para. 3.
575. *Ibid.*, Art. 3, para. 4.
576. *See* Latium Regional Administrative Court, judgment no. 7844 of 13 Jul. 2011; Council of State, judgment no. 3498 of 23 Mar. 2012. *See also* Arena, A. AGCom's Rules on Short News Reports Annulled. IRIS 1 (2012): 31 et seq., available at: http://merlin.obs.coe.int/iris/2012/1/article31.en.html; Arena, A. Council of State Upholds Annulment of AGCom's Rules on Short News Reports. IRIS 8 (2012); 30 et seq., available at: http://merlin.obs.coe.int/iris/2012/8/article30.en.html.
577. Article 3, para. 4, of Attachment A to AGCom Decision no. 667/10/CONS as amended by AGCom Decision no. 392/12/CONS.
578. *Ibid.*
579. *Ibid.*
580. *Ibid.*, Art. 4, para. 1.
581. *Ibid.*
582. *Ibid.*, Art. 4, para. 2.
583. *Ibid.*, Art. 5.

Chapter 7. Access to Networks

289. Prior to examining must-carry rules and other access obligations for networks, it is necessary to outline the rules governing the management and allocation of broadcasting frequencies. The reasons that prompted the legislature to adopt those rules include compliance with international agreements, the scarcity of broadcasting frequencies, the risk of interferences and environmental and health hazards, the need to ensure media pluralism and freedom of expression. In Italy, the management of the broadcasting spectrum takes place through a two-step process, including: (i) the Spectrum Distribution Plan and (ii) the Spectrum Allocation Plan.

290. The Spectrum Distribution Plan specifies what frequency bands each category of telecommunication services can employ.

The plan is drawn up by the Ministry of Economic Development, after consulting AGCom, the Ministries for Home Affairs, Defence, and Transports and Sustainable Mobility, the PSM provider and electronic communication operators.[584] The plan is updated every five years unless the Ministry of Economic Development deems it necessary to update the plan at an earlier date[585] to reflect developments in the field of radio broadcasting technology or in the international regulatory framework. The primary sources of the spectrum distribution plan are the International Telecommunication Union Radio Regulations, which are updated every four years.

291. The Spectrum Allocation Plan, in turn, determines the service areas, geographic location, radio-electric parameters, and the radio frequency assigned to each radio installation. In order to exclude interference with neighbouring radio-electric countries, in each coordination area defined by the international agreements signed by the Ministry of Economic Development and the authorities of the neighbouring radio-electric countries, only the frequencies allocated to Italy by the agreements themselves are subject to planning.[586]

The spectrum allocation plan is adopted by AGCom,[587] on the basis of the general criteria governing the allocation of frequencies laid down in the CLAVMS (efficiency, media pluralism, optimal coverage, preferential treatment for linguistic minorities, etc.).[588] The CLAVMS also states that, in accordance with EU law, the allocation of frequencies must be carried out according to objective, transparent, non-discriminatory and proportionate criteria.[589] The CLAVMS further provides that broadcasters must ensure efficient use of the radio frequencies assigned to them and must guarantee the integrity of their network and the quality of their signals so as to minimize the risk of interference with other radio broadcasts.[590]

584. Article 50, para. 3, CLAVMS.
585. Article 50, para. 4, CLAVMS.
586. Article 50, para. 6, CLAVMS.
587. Article 50, para. 5, CLAVMS.
588. *Ibid.*
589. Article 50, para. 2, CLAVMS.
590. Article 50, para. 1, CLAVMS.

§1. Must-Carry Rules

292. One of the aims of local broadcasting legislation is the protection and promotion of local and regional cultures. In fact, the protection of linguistic minorities is achieved by reserving a share of the total broadcasting capacity at local level for AVMS that are an expression of these linguistic minorities.[591] Moreover, the protection of local and regional cultures is also attained by reserving to the broadcasting of AVMS at local level a share of the total broadcasting capacity determined by the adoption of the frequency allocation plan for television broadcasting on terrestrial frequencies.[592] The CLAVMS provides that the AGCom shall adopt the national plan for the allocation of frequencies to be allocated to the DTT service, identifying in each technical area referred to in paragraph 1030 of Article 1 of Law No. 205 of 27 December 2017, several frequencies in the UHF band for the implementation of networks, at least one of which with coverage of not less than 90% of the population of the area, aimed at making transmission capacity available to providers of AVMS in the local area.[593] By Decision no. 39/19/CONS, the Authority adopted the National Plan for the Assignment of Frequencies to the Digital Terrestrial Television Service (NAPF). Moreover, local network operators wishing to provide transmission and distribution services to nationwide audiovisual media service providers must comply with the following restrictions: (i) the transmission capacity offered to nationwide providers must not exceed that necessary to convey two nationwide programmes for each multiplex; (ii) transmission capacity cannot be offered to nationwide content providers controlled by or connected to nationwide network providers; (iii) the transmission capacity used to convey nationwide contents must ensure coverage of at least 50% of the national population (80% after the completion of the digital switchover).[594]

293. The relationship between network operators and providers of AVMS is comprehensively regulated under AGCom Digital Broadcasting Regulation.[595]

National network operators holding rights for at least five multiplexes must offer 40% of the transmission capacity of the fifth multiplex to independent content providers.[596] Local network operators must offer a share of their transmission capacity equal to at least two programmes to local broadcasters to which no rights for the use of broadcasting frequencies have been granted.[597]

294. Except for the above requirements, the provision by network operators of transmission capacity to content providers takes place through commercial agreements, which must be notified to AGCom for prior approval.[598] Also, in the field of

591. Article 4, para. 6, CLAVMS.
592. Article 4, para. 7, CLAVMS.
593. Article 4, para. 8, CLAVMS.
594. Article 18, para. 3, of AGCom Digital Broadcasting Regulation.
595. *See* Art. 26 of AGCom Digital Broadcasting Regulation.
596. *Ibid.*, Art. 26, para. 1. *See also* AGCom Decision no. 438/13/CONS and decision no. 283/14/CONS.
597. *Ibid.*, Art. 26, para. 2.
598. *Ibid.*, Art. 26, paras 3 and 4.

radio broadcasting, the relationship between network operators and radio content providers is subject to specific rules. National network operators can offer their services only to national radio content providers.[599] Local network providers, in turn, can only provide distribution and retransmission services to local content providers.[600] Also in the field of radio broadcasting, the relationship between network operators and radio content providers is subject to specific rules. National network operators can offer their services only to national radio content providers.[601] Local network providers, in turn, can only provide distribution and retransmission services to local content providers.[602] The digital radio broadcasting regulatory framework is outlined by the Regulation on the new discipline of the start-up phase of terrestrial radio transmissions in digital mode, as per Decision no. 664/09/CONS of 26 November 2009. These rules have been subject to subsequent simplification and adjustment interventions (Decision no. 567/13/CONS and Decision no. 35/16/ CONS). With the amendments and additions to the Regulation made, most recently, by Decision no. 455/19/CONS of 27 November 2019, the Authority introduced specific rules on the conditions and procedures for access to transmission capacity by independent content providers, in order to promote the enrichment of the range of programs available to users and to ensure the development of the terrestrial radio broadcasting market in digital technology, in an open, balanced and pluralist sense.

295. The provision of transmission capacity by network operators to radio content providers is governed by contracts negotiated between those subjects.[603] Those agreements must be submitted to AGCom for prior approval.[604] In case of disputes between network operators and content providers, the Authority, in accordance with the provisions of Article 1, paragraph 11, of Law No. 249 of 31 July 1997, shall rule in accordance with the procedures set out in Decision no. 226/15/CONS.[605] The private radio network operator at national level is obliged to achieve, within two years from the assignment of the rights of use of the frequencies, homogeneous portable outdoor coverage of at least 40%, within four years of at least 60% and within five years of at least 70% of the population of the reference basin, assessed on the basis of the same technical criteria established in the planning measures.[606]

§2. OTHER ACCESS OBLIGATIONS FOR NETWORKS

296. The Italian television system officially transitioned from analogue to digital technology in 2012, after a gradual process of switching off. Digital technology entails the multiplication of transmission capacity as the electromagnetic spectrum can carry a greater number of channels, alleviating the problem of the scarcity of

599. *See* Art. 14, para. 2, of Annex A to Decision no. 664/09/CONS, of 26 Nov. 2009.
600. *Ibid*., Art. 14, para. 6.
601. *See* Art. 14, para. 2, of Annex A to Decision no. 664/09/CONS, of 26 Nov. 2009.
602. *Ibid*., Art. 14, para. 6.
603. *Ibid*., Art. 17, para. 1.
604. *Ibid*., Art. 17, para. 2.
605. *Ibid*., Art. 17, para. 1.
606. *Ibid*., Art. 14, para. 5.

broadcasting frequencies that has long characterized analogue broadcasting. The 2019 Budget Law introduced new tasks for AGCom and the Ministry of Economic Development for the purposes of implementing the process of reorganizing the radio and television system on a digital terrestrial platform, the so-called refarming of the 700 MHz band. This follows the allocation to wireless broadband (5G) electronic communication services of the frequencies in the 700 MHz band, in the implementation of Decision (EU) 2017/899 of the European Parliament and of the Council.[607]

297. In order to ensure the proper functioning of the entire process of assigning rights of use for the operation of the national networks envisaged in the Frequency Allocation Plan, AGCom has defined the criteria for converting rights of use of frequencies for the digital terrestrial service (held by national operators) into rights of use of broadcasting capacity in newly developed national multiplexes using DVB-T2 technology (Resolution No. 129/19/CONS). The DVB-T2 standard represents the second-generation technological development on the digital terrestrial platform, thanks to which spectral efficiency increases in terms of transmission capacity and therefore, with the same bandwidth, there are more TV channels or TV channels in HD quality.

298. Concerning the criteria for the complete digitization of the frequencies, as set out in Resolution 181/09/CONS, it should be noted that the same Resolution provided for the frequencies to be allocated by means of a tender procedure – that the AGCom defines as 'beauty contest' – with reservation in favour of new entrants. This was in order to comply with the commitment made to the European Commission in the process of closing infringement procedure number 2005/5086. AGCom then adopted Resolution No. 277/13/CONS for the assignment of the frequencies resulting from the so-called digital dividend, confirming the procedure for consideration set out in the aforementioned resolution for the assignment of the frequencies available in the television band for digital terrestrial broadcasting systems by Resolution No. 136/19/CONS. In this regard, it should be noted that the Italian Council of State, in its judgment of 3 October 2019, no. 6622, validated the legitimacy of Resolution No. 136/19/CONS, giving prominence to the fact that the previous Resolution No. 277/13/CONS had already been adopted as a result of interlocution with the European Commission in order to ensure, in the process of conversion to digital, the effective entry into the market of new operators, as well as the strengthening of existing small operators. In addition, the Council of State stated that AGCom, with Resolution No. 136/19/CONS – in line with Judgment No. 5929 of 16 October 2018, where the Council of State had disapplied Article 3*quinquies* of Decree-Law No. 16 of 2 March 2012, converted with amendments by Law No.

607. With this decision, the EU set 30 Jun. 2020 as the deadline for Member States to authorize the use of the 700 MHz frequency band for television systems capable of providing wireless broadband electronic communications services, subject to harmonized technical conditions. This frequency band has been allocated by auction to telephone operators. For Member States with specific needs, the deadline set by the EU is 30 June 2022. Italy has chosen to postpone the deadline to 30 June 2022, partly to ensure the natural replacement of TV sets, bearing in mind that digital terrestrial penetration is very high in our country.

44 of 26 April 2012, for infringing the EU principles of autonomy and independence of national regulatory authorities – limited itself to giving positive feedback on the suitability of the tender to ensure the participation of competitors, noting that it has in fact allowed an effective entry of new operators in the digital television market, without unduly benefiting those already present.

299. AGCom Decision no. 159/08/CONS requires RAI and Reti Televisive Italiane S.p.A. (RTI) to grant national analogue broadcasters access to their broadcasting transmission infrastructures on a transparent and non-discriminatory basis. RAI and RTI must provide a disaggregated offer of the economic and technical conditions for access to their infrastructures. RAI and RTI are also required to adopt a system of separate accounting for their analogue television broadcasting transmission services.

AGCom Decision no. 497/10/CONS, concerning the beauty contest for the awarding of the digital dividend, required Mediaset, RAI and Telecom to transfer 40% of the transmission capacity on the fifth multiplex they would have acquired via the beauty contest to independent content providers for a period of five years following the switch off.[608]

The beauty contest, however, was annulled by Decree-Law no 16 of 2 March 2012,[609] converted into law by Law no. 44 of 26 April 2012, which provided that digital terrestrial frequencies were to be awarded through an auction procedure.[610]

AGCom therefore adopted a new decision governing the auction procedure (Decision no. 277/13/CONS of 12 April 2013), which no longer set out an obligation to transfer transmission capacity, because (i) the number of frequencies to be awarded had significantly decreased and (ii) incumbent operators were excluded from the awarding procedure.[611]

Recital 93 of Decision no. 277/13/CONS, however, provided that AGCom would carry out a market analysis on the transmission capacity market so as to determine whether transfer obligations were required. AGCom launched that analysis in Decision no. 438/13/CONS.[612]

608. AGCom Decision no. 497/10/CONS.
609. Decree-Law of 2 Mar. 2012, no. 16.
610. *See* s. 3*quinquies* of Law 26 Apr. 2012, no. 44.
611. AGCom Decision no. 277/13/CONS.
612. AGCom Decision no. 438/13/CONS.

Chapter 8. Standards and Interoperability

300. The Electronic Communications Code regards interoperability between electronic communications networks and services as one of the aims of electronic communications legislation.[613] The regulation of those services and networks conforms to the technical standards and regulations set at the EU level, as well as the recommendations issued by bodies established by international agreements to which Italy is a party.[614]

301. Those statements are fleshed out by Article 13 of the Electronic Communications Code, which entrusts the Ministry of Economic Development and AGCom to promote the establishment and development of interoperability and consistent practices and standards in the implementation of the Code.[615]

In the performance of those tasks, the Ministry of Economic Development is assisted by the Superior Information and Communication Technology Institute.[616] The latter is a member, along with the Italian Electrotechnical Committee[617] and the Italian Unification Body,[618] of the National Coordination Committee for Information and Communications. The Superior Information and Communication Technology Institute, most notably, drafted several technical specifications for interconnection in the field of electronic communications.[619]

302. As far as standardization is concerned, the Ministry of Economic Development supervises the implementation of technical specifications and standards published in the Official Journal of the European Union (OJEU) for the harmonized provision of services, technical interfaces, and network protocols, so as to ensure interoperability of services and to broaden users' freedom of choice.[620]

Pending the adoption of harmonized standards by the European Commission, the Ministry of Economic Development promotes the implementation of technical specifications and standards developed by European standardization bodies or, failing that, by the International Telecommunication Union, the International Organization for Standardization, and the International Electrotechnical Commission.[621]

613. *See* Art. 4, para. 3, letter (g) of the Electronic Communications Code.
614. *Ibid.*, Art. 4, para. 4.
615. *Ibid.*, Art. 13, para. 5, letters (c) and (e).
616. www.isticom.it/.
617. www.ceiweb.it/.
618. www.uni.com/.
619. www.isticom.it/index.php/specifiche-tecniche#specinter.
620. *Ibid.*, Art. 20, para. 1.
621. *Ibid.*, Art. 20, para. 2.

Part IV. Cross-Ownership Regulation

303. As noted in Part I, the principle of media pluralism is one of the foremost constitutional values in the regulation of media matters.[622] The external dimension of pluralism, in particular, entails the availability of as many information sources as possible, having regard to the current state of technical development.

The Constitutional Court has consistently held that media pluralism is essential for a truly democratic polity and has repeatedly called upon the legislature to lay down rules to prevent the concentration of market power in the hands of a limited number of subjects.[623]

The legislature and the Government, in turn, have often lagged behind in addressing the issue of media concentration. Moreover, a number of laws seeking to regulate that matter were struck down by the Constitutional Court as the latter deemed those laws unable to ensure a sufficient degree of pluralism, notably in the broadcasting sector.[624]

Cross-ownership regulation in Italy currently takes the form of horizontal concentration rules and sector-specific rules for broadcasting and press.

General principles of the system of audiovisual media and radio services to safeguard pluralism and competition are set out in Article 5 CLAVMS. It provides for a general authorization regime for the activities of network operators or of providers of associated interactive services or conditional access services.[625] This regime does not involve the assignment of radio frequencies, which shall be conferred with a separate act.[626]

622. *See*, for example, Constitutional Court, Judgment no. 153 of 1987; no. 826 of 1988; no. 420 of 1994; no. 155 of 2002; no. 466 of 2002.
623. Judgment no. 420/94, where the Court stated that any absence or shortcomings of external pluralism, due to the lack of effective antitrust provisions, cannot be compensated by the presence of a public service broadcaster whose primary commitment is to ensure that internal pluralism is safeguarded.
624. *See*, for example, Constitutional Court, Judgment no. 420 of 1994 (holding that Art. 15, para. 4, of the Mammì law was unconstitutional in that it allowed the same broadcaster to hold up to 25% of the available broadcasting frequencies and up to three broadcasting networks); Judgment no. 466 of 2002 (holding that Art. 3, para. 7, of the Maccanico law was unconstitutional in that it did not set out a clear deadline for the transitional period during which broadcasters exceeding the concentration limits could carry on broadcasting their programmes).
625. Article 5, para. 1, letter (b) CLAVMS.
626. Article 5, para. 3 CLAVMS.

§1. Horizontal Rules for the Integrated Communications System

304. The most relevant media concentration rules are set out in Article 51 CLAVMS, which refers to the notion of ICS.

The ICS is the economic sector defined by the law encompassing the following activities: daily and periodical press, press agencies, electronic publishing, including Internet publishing, radio and AVMS, cinema, external advertising, sponsorship and online advertising.[627]

Several scholarly commentators have criticized the ICS as being too large and as comprising heterogeneous services.[628]

305. The CLAVMS prohibits holding positions of significant market power detrimental to pluralism in the ICS and in its constituent submarkets.[629]

Moreover, according to CLAVMS AGCom shall monitor the performance and evolution of the ICS and shall ascertain, at least once a year, by publishing the results, its overall economic value and that of its constituent submarkets, also giving evidence of the positions of market power of the subjects active in these markets and the potential risks for pluralism.[630] For the purposes of these quantifications, the revenues earned in Italy, including by companies based abroad, are taken into account. Such revenues include, *inter alia*, those derived from the sale of daily newspapers and periodicals, online publishing, advertising, teleshopping, sponsorships and so forth.[631]

306. The enforcement of the prohibitions related to holding positions of significant market power detrimental to pluralism in the ICS and in its constituent submarkets is entrusted to AGCom.[632] To facilitate AGCom's enforcement tasks, all companies active in the ICS are required to notify agreements and mergers to AGCom.[633] Notification procedures are defined in specific regulations adopted by AGCom.[634]

AGCom adopts every year a decision setting out an estimate of the overall ICS revenues.[635] If AGCom establishes a breach of the prohibitions set out in Article 51 CLAVMS, it must take appropriate measures to ensure that those breaches are remedied in a timely fashion.[636]

627. Article 3 para. 1, letter (z) of CLAVMS.
628. *See* R. Zaccaria, A. Valastro, E. Albanesi, *Diritto dell'informazione e della comunicazione*, (Padua: Cedam, 2021); R. Mastroianni, *Riforma del sistema radiotelevisivo italiano e diritto europeo* (Turin: Giappichelli 2004), 63.
629. Article 51, para. 1, CLAVMS.
630. Article 51, para. 2, CLAVMS.
631. Article 51, para. 2, CLAVMS.
632. Article 51, para. 5, CLAVMS.
633. Article 51, para. 3, CLAVMS.
634. Article 51, para. 4, CLAVMS.
635. *Ibid.*
636. Article 51, para. 6, CLAVMS.

§2. Sector-Specific Rules for the Broadcasting Sector

307. The CLAVMS deleted the specific 'technical' limits that were set out for the broadcasting sector. Nowadays, the holders of authorizations permitting the broadcasting of more than 20% of the total television programmes or more than 20% of the radio programmes irradiated on terrestrial frequencies at national level by means of the networks envisaged in the national plan for the assignment of television frequencies in digital technique are bound by the above-mentioned obligation of notification to AGCom.[637]

§3. Sector-Specific Rules for the Press Sector

308. Turning to the press sector, Law no. 416/81, as amended by Law no. 67/87, sets out a ban on the holding of a dominant position in the daily newspaper publishing market.[638]

For the purpose of that ban, the notion of dominant position is defined by reference to the share of the total circulation of daily newspapers in Italy or one of the four inter-regional areas defined by the law.[639]

Transactions leading to the creation of a dominant position are null and void[640] and can result in the compulsory sale of shares or newspapers so as to eliminate the dominant position.[641]

309. The CLAVMS provides that operators who earn revenues exceeding 8% of the total revenues of the ICS and who at the same time have or acquire shareholdings in companies publishing daily newspapers, with the exception of companies publishing daily newspapers distributed exclusively by electronic means, are bound by the above-mentioned obligation of notification to AGCom.[642]

310. Also, advertising in the daily newspaper publishing sector is subject to specific restrictions. Law no. 416/1981 stipulates that no advertising agency can enter into exclusive dealing arrangements with a number of daily newspapers whose combined circulation exceeds 30% of the total nationwide circulation.[643] The applicable threshold drops to 20% for advertising agencies having corporate connections with publishers.[644]

637. Article 51, para. 3, letter (d), CLAVMS.
638. Law 5 Aug. 1981, no. 416; Law 25 Feb. 1987, no. 67.
639. *Ibid.*, Art. 3(1).
640. *Ibid.*, Art. 3(4).
641. *Ibid.*, Art. 3(5)–(6).
642. Article 51, para. 3, letter (c), CLAVMS.
643. Law no. 416/81, Art. 12(3).
644. *Ibid.*, Art. 12(4).

Part V. Supervision: Media Regulator

311. In Italy, supervision tasks in the field of media are concentrated in AGCom, the Italian Communications Regulation Authority. Before turning to AGCom, however, regard must be had to the other two bodies with which AGCom shares its supervision and regulatory powers: the Ministry of Economic Development (Directorate-General for Electronic communications, Radio broadcasting, and Postal services, DGERP) and the PSC.

§1. The Ministry of Economic Development

312. The Ministry of Communications was established in 1993 to replace the Ministry of Post and Telecommunications. In 2008, it was merged into the Ministry of Economic Development. All competences formerly exercised by the Ministry of Communications were entrusted to the Department of Communications within the Ministry of Economic Development, chaired by a Vice-Minister. In December 2013, a Decree of the President of the Council of Ministers revised the internal organization of the Ministry of Economic Development.[645] Departments were abolished and fifteen Directorates-General (DGs) were set up under the aegis of a Secretariat General. Competences in the field of media and communications are attributed to the DGERP, which comprises several divisions.

313. The Ministry of Economic Development currently has a significant role in the field of AVMS, although the Constitutional Court urged on several occasions that the Parliament be granted a dominant role in this matter, as it is better situated at protecting media pluralism and other constitutional values.[646]

The Ministry of Economic Development relies upon the Supervision Committee of the 'Media and Minors' Self-regulation Code.[647]

314. After the establishment of AGCom in 1997, several attempts have been made at clarifying the division of tasks between AGCom and the Ministry of Communications.[648] At the outset, without prejudice to powers entrusted to the Ministry

645. Decree of the President of the Council of Ministers of 5 Dec. 2013, no. 158.
646. *See* Constitutional Court, Judgment no. 225 of 1974.
647. Article 8, para. 2, CLAVMS.
648. *See* generally O. Grandinetti, 'Il riparto di attribuzioni tra Autorità per le garanzie nelle comunicazioni e Ministero nella gestione delle radiofrequenze', *Costituzionalismo.it* (2004): 6 et seq.

by earlier legislation,[649] the Ministry was required to assist AGCom in the exercise of its competences.[650] In particular, the Ministry was entrusted with regulatory and administrative functions (frequency planning, issuance of authorizations, sanctioning powers) and with the task of supervising the public service broadcaster, while AGCom was endowed with regulatory powers in the field of broadcasting.

Legislative Decree no. 366/2003 redefined the division of tasks between AGCom and the Ministry. The latter was empowered to implement policies in the field of communications; to regulate electronic communications, audiovisual media and radio services; to manage and assign broadcasting frequencies; to issue authorization and licences to media operators; to monitor compliance with universal services obligations; to promote research in the field of information technology and multimedia services.[651] In sum, the powers of the Ministry have gradually expanded to the expense of AGCom's competences.[652] This outcome is at variance with the trend at the EU level, where independent authorities have a pivotal role. More recently, with the Electronic Communications Code, the ministerial offices have been transferred back powers relating to measures concerning electronic communications networks and services, rights of use and numbering, leaving AGCom with regulatory powers in the strict sense of the term, particularly in the area of interconnection and access.[653]

315. The current attributions of the Ministry of Economic Development are spelled out in the CLAVMS, which recalls some of the provisions of Legislative Decree no. 366/2003. The Ministry of Economic Development has relevant administrative powers in the context of the management of the radio spectrum, as it adopts the Spectrum Distribution Plan after consulting AGCom, the Ministries of Internal Affairs, Defence, Infrastructure and Sustainable Mobility, the PSM operator and the electronic communications operators.[654]

316. The Ministry of Economic Development's main administrative powers concern the issuance of the authorizations required to access the activities of audiovisual media and radio service providers[655] as well as of electronic communications operators.[656] The Ministry, moreover, is responsible for issuing authorizations

649. Decree-Law no. 487 of 1 Dec. 1993.
650. Article 1, para. 25 of the Maccanico Law.
651. Article 2 of Legislative Decree no. 366 of 3 Dec. 2003.
652. *See* G. Gardini, *Le Regole dell'Informazione. Verso la Gigabit Society* (Turin: Giappichelli, 2021); R. Zaccaria, A. Valastro, E. Albanesi, *Diritto dell'informazione e della comunicazione*, (Padua: Cedam, 2021).
653. *See* Art. 29 CLAVMS.
654. Article 50, para. 3, CLAVMS.
655. *See,* for example, Art. 13, para. 3, CLAVMS (concerning digital terrestrial network operators); Art. 14, para. 1, CLAVMS (concerning digital terrestrial audiovisual media providers); Arts 3, para. 1; 10 para. 1, and 12, para. 2 of the Regulation appearing in Annex A to AGCom Decision no. 664/09/CONS (concerning, respectively, radio content providers, service providers, and network operators).
656. Article 25 of the Electronic Communications Code.

enabling specific forms of exercise of those activities, such as the interconnection between local broadcasters,[657] the modification of broadcasting installations,[658] spectrum trading,[659] etc.

The Ministry, moreover, holds supervision and sanctioning powers in its competence areas. For instance, it may withdraw authorizations[660] and seize broadcasting installations using radio frequencies without authorization.[661]

The Ministry of Economic Development exercises significant powers also vis-à-vis the PSM provider: it concludes the service contract with RAI[662] and adopts, jointly with AGCom, the guidelines specifying the contents of the new service contract prior to its renewal.[663]

§2. The Parliamentary Supervision Committee

317. The Parliamentary Committee for the Direction and Supervision of Public Service Broadcasting (*Commissione Parlamentare per l'indirizzo e la vigilanza del servizio pubblico radiotelevisivo,* hereafter: the 'PSC'),[664] was established by Law no. 103 of 1975,[665] following calls from the Constitutional Court for a shift in broadcasting governance from the executive to the Parliament.[666]

The PSC consists of twenty Members of the Chamber of Deputies and twenty Senators appointed by the Chairs of both Houses on the basis of the Parliamentary groups' designations.[667]

318. PSC's tasks include direction powers, so as to ensure that the PSM operator conforms to the fundamental principles governing the broadcasting sector, namely, independence, objectivity and a pluralistic attitude towards diverse cultural, social and political views.[668] The PSC, in particular, may issue directives to the PSM operator as to its investment and expenditure plans, its programme schedule, and its advertising policy.[669]

319. The 2015 law reforming RAI has confirmed the Commission's general policy-making and supervisory functions in relation to public broadcasting services, but it has removed its economic-management policy-making powers, which were based on the indication of general criteria for the formation of RAI's annual and

657. Article 26, CLAVMS.
658. Article 25, para. 1, CLAVMS.
659. Article 14, paras 3–5 of the Electronic Communications Code.
660. Article 68 CLAVMS.
661. Article 102, para. 7, of the Electronic Communications Code.
662. Article 59, para. 1, CLAVMS.
663. *Ibid.*, para. 6.
664. *See* F. Bruno, G. Nava, *Il nuovo ordinamento delle comunicazioni. Radiotelevisione, comunicazionioni elettroniche, editoria* (Milan: Giuffrè, 2006), 139 et seq.
665. Articles 1 and 5 of Law 14 Apr. 1975, no. 103.
666. Constitutional Court, Judgment no. 225 of 1974.
667. Article 1 of Law no. 103 of 1975.
668. *See* Articles from 4 to 6 CLAVMS.
669. Article 4 of Law 103 of 1975.

multi-annual expenditure and investment plans. The Commission's competence to supervise the implementation of the annual and multi-annual programming plans and the compliance of the programmes transmitted with the guidelines has been eliminated; these functions are currently attributed to RAI's top management. The reform has also abrogated the competence in the formulation of the general guidelines concerning advertising messages, and the powers of a political-administrative nature concerning the indication of the members of Rai's board of directors have been taken away from the commission (the expression of the two-thirds majority opinion on the choice of the President, pursuant to Article 63, paragraph 14, CLAVMS, still stands). The PSC, moreover, is endowed with regulatory powers. Apart from adopting its own rules of procedure,[670] the PSC may regulate the access to the transmission time that the PSM operator must reserve for political parties.[671] Law no. 28 of 2000, moreover, empowered the PSC to lay down regulations to implement the legislative framework on political communication in respect of the PSM operator (AGCom has a similar power vis-à-vis commercial broadcasters).[672]

320. Turning to PSC's consultative powers, it is worth reminding that the PSC gives its opinions on PSM operator's statute and service contract,[673] and on the programmes addressed to other countries for the promotion of the Italian language and culture.[674]

Last, the PSC has information and investigation powers, which are instrumental to the exercise of the other powers outlined in this section. The PSC can invite for an audition RAI's President, directors, general manager, executives, as well as anyone who may provide useful information.[675] The PSC can ask the PSM provider to produce documents and carry out surveys and inquiries.[676]

670. The latest version of the PSC's rules of procedure is available at: http://parlamento17.camera.it/134.
671. Article 6 of Law no. 103 of 14 Apr. 1975.
672. Article 2, para. 5, of Law 22 Feb. 2000, no. 28.
673. Article 1, para. 6, letter (b), n. 10 of the Maccanico Law.
674. Article 19, letter (b) of the Maccanico Law.
675. Article 4 of Law no. 103 of 1975.
676. *Ibid.*

Chapter 1. AGCom's Organization

321. AGCom, the Italian Communications Regulation Authority (*Autorità per le Garanzie nelle Comunicazioni*) was established by Law 31 July 1997, no. 249 as an independent authority entrusted with regulatory and monitoring powers in the fields of AVMS, electronic communications and publishing.

AGCom's status as an 'independent authority' implies that it is not accountable to the Government and that it should not be subject to any sort of political influence.[677]

322. AGCom consists of four different bodies: the President, the Council, the Commission for Services and Products (hereafter: CSP) and the Commission for Infrastructures and Networks (hereafter: CIN).[678] The Council is composed of the President and 4 Commissioners (also known as AGCom 'Members'); the CSP and the CIN are each composed of the President and two Commissioners.

The President's task is to promote and coordinate AGCom's activities.[679] The President represents the Authority, convenes its bodies, sets their agendas, chairs meetings and monitors the implementation of AGCom Resolutions.

The President is designated by the Italian Prime Minister, upon agreement with the Minister for Economic Development. The appointment of AGCom's President takes the form of a decree of the President of the Republic, which requires approval by a two-thirds majority by the relevant Parliamentary committees. The President's term of office is seven years. He or she cannot be re-elected. The remaining four AGCom Members are appointed by the Parliament, two by the Chamber of Deputies and two by the Senate. Each Member of Parliament casts his or her vote by indicating one name: the purpose of the limited vote is to ensure a substantial balance between majority and opposition. In addition, the number of AGCom commissioners was reduced from eight to four, excluding the president, by Article 23 of Law Decree no. 201 of 2011, with a view to limiting public expenditure.

323. Law 14 November 1995, no. 481 sets out the eligibility requirements, cases of incompatibility, confidentiality obligations and remuneration of AGCom Members.

To be eligible, AGCom Members must be endowed with undisputed expertise and competence in the relevant sector.

AGCom Members cannot exercise, directly or indirectly, consultancy or professional activities, be managers or employees of public and private entities, hold public offices of any nature, including positions in political parties, or have any interest, direct or indirect, in any undertakings active in the sector within the purview of AGCom. Public servants are suspended from their functions for the duration of their

677. For an in-depth assessment of AGCom's independence, *see* INDIREG, Preliminary final report, 285–287, available at: http://ec.europa.eu/avpolicy/docs/library/studies/regulators/ preliminary_final_report.pdf.
678. Article 1, para. 3 of the Maccanico Law.
679. Article 3 of AGCom Decision no. 316/02/CONS, as subsequently amended.

term as AGCom Members. Former AGCom Members are prohibited from accepting, for a period of four years from their last day in office, employment positions or consultancy offers from undertakings active in the matters subject to AGCom's powers.

AGCom Members are subject to a number of general obligations: a duty of confidentiality (that also applies to AGCom officials); the obligations set out in the law governing administrative action (Law no. 241/1990); the division of powers among public servants.

324. AGCom's auxiliary bodies include the National Council of Users and Regional Communication Committees. The 'National Council of Users' (*Consiglio nazionale degli utenti,* hereinafter: 'NCU') was established by the Maccanico Law as AGCom's auxiliary body.[680] The NCU replaced the Consultative Council of Users established by the Mammì Law as an auxiliary body of the Broadcasting and Publishing Supervisory Board (*Garante per la radiodiffusione e l'editoria*).[681]

The NCU may issue various types of acts, including proposals and recommendations. Those acts may be addressed both to regulation and supervision bodies (e.g., the Parliament, AGCom, the Ministry of Economic Development) and to communication operators.[682]

The NCU is composed of experts, designated by associations representing various categories of users, who distinguished themselves for their role in the defence of human dignity and the protection of minors.[683]

325. Regional Communication Committees (*Comitati regionali per le comunicazioni*, hereinafter 'CORECOMs') were established by the Maccanico Law[684] to address the need for greater decentralization of AGCom's tasks and promote devolution of media governance at the local level.

CORECOMs are established in each Italian Region and exercise both the powers directly entrusted to them by national or regional laws and the powers delegated to them by AGCom by way of ad hoc conventions. Delegated powers, to date, include monitoring compliance by local communications operators with the rules on the protection of minors, on the disclosure of polls and surveys, on the exercise of the right of reply; the power to resolve disputes between local communication operators and users; the task of administering the Communication Operators Registry at the regional level.[685]

AGCom, with its own regulation, set the eligibility requirements for CORECOM Members, their incompatibilities and the organizational and funding arrangements.[686] CORECOMs are financed both by the Regions (for the exercise of tasks having a Regional relevance) and by AGCom (for the exercise of powers delegated

680. *See* Art. 1, para. 28 of the Maccanico Law.
681. *See* Art. 28 of the Mammì Law.
682. *See* Art. 1, para. 28 of the Maccanico Law.
683. *Ibid.*
684. Article 1, para. 13 of the Maccanico Law.
685. R. Zaccaria, A. Valastro, E. Albanesi, *Diritto dell'informazione e della comunicazione* (Padua: Cedam, 2021).
686. AGCom Decisions no. 52 and 53 of 1999.

by AGCom).[687] In exercising their functions, CORECOMs are assisted by an independent body, whose composition is determined by Regional legislation in accordance with AGCom.[688]

326. Initially, AGCom was supposed to autonomously manage its appropriation within the framework of a dedicated endowment of the State budget.[689]

Law no. 266 of 23 December 2005 ('Budget Law 2006') replaced the said appropriation (about EUR 20 million) with an endowment of only EUR 3 million. AGCom, however, was also authorized to impose a fee on undertakings subject to its regulatory oversight up to 0.2% of their revenues.

Scholarly commentators have highlighted the significant risk of regulatory capture inherent in that financing mechanism,[690] which has also been criticized by the regulated undertakings for the amount of the fee. In that respect, in July 2013, the ECJ ruled that Directive 2002/20/EC must be interpreted as meaning that it does not preclude a financing scheme for National Regulation Authorities based on a charge paid by the electronic communication industry provided that: (i) the charge is exclusively intended to cover the costs relating to the activities incurred by that authority for the purposes of the regulation *ex ante* of the market which leads to the grant of authorizations as per Directive 2002/20/EC, (ii) that the totality of the income obtained in respect of that charge does not exceed the total costs relating to those activities, and (iii) that that charge is imposed upon individual undertakings in an objective, transparent and proportionate manner.[691] Accordingly, in January 2014, the Latium Regional Administrative Court determined that AGCom's financing mechanism failed to meet the three above requirements, in that it was designed to cover also costs unrelated to the regulation of electronic communications, it allowed AGCom to turn a profit for several successive years, and it failed to comply with the principle of proportionality.[692]

In 2020, the Court of Justice gave a preliminary ruling on the interpretation of Directive 2002/20 in the context of a lawsuit involving AGCom. In particular, the Court of Justice ruled that Article 12(1)(a) of that Directive must be interpreted as meaning that the costs which may be covered by a charge imposed on electronic communications operators are only those relating to three categories of national regulatory authority activities (i.e., regulatory, supervisory, dispute-resolution and penalty-imposing tasks) and are not limited to costs arising from the activity of *ex ante* market regulation. The Court of Justice also ruled that Article 12(2) of Directive 2002/20 must be interpreted as not precluding provisions, such as those in force in Italy, under which: (i) the yearly overview is published after the end of the

687. Article 1, letter (B) para. (3) of AGCom Decision no. 52/99/CONS.
688. Article 1, letter (B) para. (4) of AGCom Decision no. 52/99/CONS.
689. Article 1, para. 9, of the Maccanico Law.
690. R. Zaccaria, A. Valastro, E. Albanesi, *Diritto dell'informazione e della comunicazione*, (Padua: Cedam, 2021).
691. ECJ, Joined Cases C-228/12 to C-232/12 and C-254/12 to C-258/12, *Vodafone Omnitel NV et a.*, [2014], *nyr.*
692. Latium Regional Administrative Court, Judgment no. 2534/2014.

financial year in which the administrative charges are levied, and (ii) the appropriate adjustments are made in a financial year which does not immediately follow the year in which the charges were levied.

Chapter 2. Tasks

327. The Maccanico Law entrusted AGCom with tasks and powers formerly exercised by the Broadcasting and Publishing Supervisory Board (*Garante per la radiodiffusione e l'editoria*)[693] as well as with new attributions. Those tasks are currently shared by AGCom's CSP, CIN, and Council as outlined in §1 below. AGCom also holds some powers in the antitrust domains. The division of tasks between AGCom and the Italian Antitrust Authority is addressed in §2 below.

§1. The Internal Division of Tasks Between AGCom's CSP, CIN, and Council

328. AGCom's CSP monitors compliance by the products and services offered by communication operators with legal standards and requirements;[694] it issues guidelines setting minimum quality standards for communication services;[695] it monitors the distribution of services and products, including their advertising, without prejudice to the enforcement powers in the field of misleading advertising entrusted to the Italian Antitrust Authority.[696]

The CSP also ensures compliance with the window periods for the exploitation of audiovisual works;[697] it adopts regulations in the fields of advertising and teleshopping to implement statutory provisions;[698] it monitors compliance with the statutory and self-regulation rules concerning the protection of minors and imposes sanctions for the infringement thereof.[699]

The CSP, moreover, monitors compliance with the rules on the protection of linguistic minorities,[700] the right to reply,[701] political communication,[702] and the publication of polls and surveys.[703] Last but not least, it checks whether the PSM operator complies with its remit as set out in the service contract.[704]

329. AGCom's CIN is responsible for the management of the radio spectrum, the regulation of interconnection and access to telecommunications infrastructures, and the definition of the subjective and objective elements of the universal service.[705]

693. Article 1, para. 6, letter (c), no. 9 of the Maccanico Law.
694. *Ibid.,* letter (b), no. 1.
695. *Ibid.*, no. 2.
696. *Ibid.*, no. 3.
697. *Ibid.*, no. 4.
698. *Ibid.*, no. 5.
699. *Ibid.*, no. 6.
700. *Ibid.*, no. 7.
701. *Ibid.*, no. 8.
702. *Ibid.*, no. 9.
703. *Ibid.*, no. 12.
704. *Ibid.*, no. 10. *See also* Art. 62, para. 1, CLAVMS.
705. *See* R. Zaccaria, A. Valastro, E. Albanesi, *Diritto dell'informazione e della comunicazione*, (Padua: Cedam, 2021).

As to the management of the radio spectrum, CIN's competences coexist with those of AGCom's Council. The CIN has the power to monitor compliance with the radiofrequency caps designed to protect human health[706] and provide the Ministry of Economic Development with an opinion on the scheme of the national Spectrum Distribution Plan.[707]

The CIN may adopt measures to ensure the safety of communications and to avoid electromagnetic interferences, also by requiring the modification of broadcasting installations.[708] The CIN also sets the standards for decoders, in order to promote the availability of communication services.[709]

The CIN, moreover, defines objective and transparent criteria, as well as price caps, for interconnection and access to telecommunication infrastructures;[710] it oversees the relations between infrastructure operators and users and ensures that the former grant the latter interconnection and access to infrastructures;[711] it settles disputes related to interconnection and access matters.[712]

The CIN defines the subjective and objective scope of universal service obligations and their compensation in accordance with EU and national legislation.[713]

330. AGCom's Council, which consists of the AGCom President and all AGCom Commissioners, exercises, apart from the tasks expressly entrusted to it, all the powers not conferred to the CSP or the CIN.[714]

The Council may solicit the Government to take measures, even of a legislative nature, to reflect the technical and legal developments of the communications sector;[715] it monitors the application of legislation governing the access to communication infrastructures, also through specific regulations;[716] it promotes research in the field of communication technology and multimedia services.[717]

Turning to the matter of authorizations, the Council adopts a regulation setting out the relevant requirements and fees;[718] it drafts protocols on behalf of the Ministry of Economic Development for the issuance of those authorizations;[719] it audits the budgets and information provided by authorization recipients.[720]

The Council also holds powers in antitrust matters: it establishes the existence of dominant positions in the audiovisual sector and adopts the necessary measures.[721]

706. Article 1, para. 6, letter (a), no. 15 of the Maccanico Law.
707. *Ibid.*, no. 2.
708. *Ibid.*, no. 3.
709. *Ibid.*, no. 4.
710. *Ibid.*, no. 7.
711. *Ibid.*, no. 8.
712. *Ibid.*, no. 9.
713. *Ibid.*, no. 11.
714. *Ibid.*, letter (c), no. 7.
715. Article 1, para. 6, letter (c), no. 1 of the Maccanico Law.
716. *Ibid.*, no. 2.
717. *Ibid.*, no. 3.
718. *Ibid.*, no. 5.
719. *Ibid.*, no. 6.
720. *Ibid.*, no. 7.
721. *Ibid.*, no. 2.

The Council, moreover, monitors compliance by the PSM provider with the directives issued by the Parliamentary Committee for the Steering and Supervision of Broadcasting and prompts the PSM provider to open disciplinary proceedings against responsible executives.[722]

The Council must, by 30 June of each year, submit a report on AGCom's activities to the President of the Council of Ministers, which forwards it to the Parliament. This report must specify facts and figures for each area of AGCom competence concerning, *inter alia*, technical development, resources, revenues, audience shares, cross-shareholdings among radio, television, and press and so forth.[723]

Last, the Council administers the Register of Communication Operators, where recipients of authorizations, communication operators, advertising concessionaires, publishing companies, and news agencies are registered.[724]

§2. The Division of Powers Between AGCom and the Italian Antitrust Authority

331. The entrustment to AGCom of attributions in the antitrust domain, albeit only in the context of media markets, calls for principles to coordinate AGCom's action with that of another independent body: the Italian Antitrust Authority (*Autorità garante della concorrenza e del mercato*).

332. By and large, it is possible to mark a distinction between the tasks of those two authorities in accordance with the constitutional values each of them pursues: AGCom is responsible for the protection of media pluralism and for the broadest possible dissemination of ideas; the Antitrust Authority, instead, is accountable for the safeguard the freedom of enterprise and a workable competition in the market.

Accordingly, AGCom monitors the creation of dominant positions in the media markets, as the very existence of such positions can harm the pluralism of information and media. In contrast, the Antitrust Authority only comes into play when undertakings abuse their dominant positions to distort competition.[725]

333. In order to promote consistency between the action of those authorities, Law no. 249/1997 requires the Antitrust Authority to seek an opinion from AGCom before exercising its powers vis-à-vis undertakings operating in the communications sector.[726]

722. *Ibid.*, no. 10.
723. *Ibid.*, no. 12.
724. Article 1, para. 6, letter (a) n. 5 of the Maccanico Law.
725. R. Zaccaria, A. Valastro, E. Albanesi, *Diritto dell'informazione e della comunicazione* (Padua: Cedam, 2021).
726. Law no. 249/97, Art. 1, para. 11.

Chapter 3. Sanctioning Powers

334. As a part of its supervision tasks, AGCom holds a broad scope of sanctioning powers. In order to ensure the right of defence set out in the Constitution, addresses of AGCom decisions imposing sanctions can challenge those decisions before the Latium Regional Administrative Court and can appeal the judgments of those courts before the Council of State.

335. Sanctions usually are of a pecuniary nature and are either determined by AGCom within the minimum and maximum amounts predetermined by the law[727] or are calculated as a percentage of the offending company's turnover.[728]

In specific fields, such as cross-ownership and concentration rules, AGCom may also issue injunctions and other structural remedies.[729]

336. The procedural arrangements governing the exercise by AGCom of its sanctioning powers are currently laid down in AGCom Decision no. 410/14/CONS. The resolution approves the new Regulation on administrative sanctions and commitments, which governs the pre-investigation and preliminary investigation activities aimed at exercising AGCom's power to impose pecuniary administrative sanctions in accordance with the principles set out in Law no. 689 of 24 November 1981 on administrative sanctions, and the institution of commitments. The text of the Regulations – which replaced the previous Regulations set out in Resolution No. 136/06/CONS – was subsequently amended by Annex A to Resolution No. 529/14/CONS and Annex A to Resolution No. 581/15/CONS. The amendments made by Resolution No. 581/15/CONS came into force on 1 January 2016.

All interested subjects, such as users, consumer associations, and law enforcement agencies, may request AGCom to institute proceedings to establish a breach of media legislation and to impose sanctions on the offending operators. Moreover, AGCom may start investigations and impose sanctions *motu proprio*.

337. Upon the opening of an investigation, the individual or entity suspected of a breach must be notified of a notice setting out a summary of the alleged violations, as well as the relevant steps to request a hearing and to submit observations and documents. Investigations must, as a rule, be completed within 150 days of the notification of the said notice, but may be extended in specified cases.

338. If AGCom determines that a violation of media legislation has taken place, it must notify the wrongdoer of its decision, along with a detailed statement of the grounds and the deadline to challenge that decision before administrative courts.

727. *See*, for example, Art. 67, para. 2, CLAVMS.

728. *See*, for example, Art. 62, para. 8, CLAVMS (providing that AGCom may impose a sanction up to 3% of the public service media operator's turnover in case that company fails to meet its public service remit).

729. *See* Art. 51, para. 6 CLAVMS (empowering AGCom to require the divestiture of companies or branches to secure compliance with the relevant media concentration limits).

Chapter 4. Procedures for Extrajudicial Settlement of Disputes

339. Article 40 CLAVMS provides that the AGCom shall define by regulation transparent, non-discriminatory and easily accessible procedures for the settlement of disputes between users and providers of AVMS addressed to the Italian public.[730] AGCom monitors these procedures.[731]

This is without prejudice to the right to appeal to the competent court for the purposes of judicial settlement of the dispute.[732]

340. Pursuant to Article 40 CLAMVS, the AGCom adopted Resolution No. 358/22/CONS amending the dispute-resolution procedures for AVMS. The new procedures apply from 1 February 2023. In a nutshell, the AGCom has provided that the existing two-step procedure for electronic communications (which provides for an attempt at conciliation and, in the event of a negative outcome, the possibility of access to a decision-making procedure) will be also applied to disputes between users and providers of AVMS, albeit with some differences. In particular, for disputes concerning AVMS, the attempt at conciliation will not be a condition for proceeding to court (so-called mandatory attempt at conciliation). The management of the entire procedure, including the conciliation phase, will be the responsibility of AGCom. The dispute-resolution procedures will take place through the ConciliaWeb platform.

730. Article 40, para. 1 CLAVMS.
731. Article 40, para. 5 CLAVMS.
732. Article 40, para. 3 CLAVMS.

Selected Bibliography

Apa, E. *La pubblicità commerciale.* Napoli: Iovene, 2010.

Arena, A. 'The ECJ as Agenda Setter in European Audiovisual Media Policy'. In *The Palgrave Handbook of European Media Policy,* edited by K. Donders, C. Pauwels & J. Loisen, Houndmills. Basingstoke, Hampshire: Palgrave Macmillan, 2014, 218–238.

Bassan, F. & E. Tosi. *Diritto degli audiovisivi.* Milan: Giuffré, 2012.

Barile, P. *Libertà di manifestazione del pensiero.* Milan: Giuffrè, 1975.

Bruno, F. & G. Nava. *Il nuovo ordinamento delle comunicazioni. Radiotelevisione, comunicazionioni elettroniche, editoria.* Milan: Giuffrè, 2006.

Caretti, P. *Diritto dell'informazione e della comunicazione: stampa, radiotelevisione, telecomunicazioni, teatro e cinema.* Bologna: Il Mulino, 2013.

Caretti, P. (ed.). *L'informazione. Il percorso di una libertà*, Vol. II. Firenze: Passigli, 2012.

Contessa, C. & Del Vecchio, P. (eds), Testo unico dei servizi di media audiovisivi e radiofonici – Il D.l.vo 31 luglio 2005, n. 177 – TUSMAR, La Tribuna, 2021.

Costanzo, P., G. De Minico & R. Zaccaria (eds). *I 'tre codici' della società dell'informazione: amministrazione digitale, comunicazioni elettroniche e contenuti audiovisivi.* Turin: Giappichelli, 2006.

Donati, F. L'art. 21 della Costituzione settanta anni dopo, *in Rivista del diritto dei media* (2018): 1 et seq.

Esposito, C. *La libertà di manifestazione del pensiero nell'ordinamento italiano.* Milano: Giuffré, 1958.

Gardini, G. *Le Regole dell'Informazione. Verso la Gigabit Society*, Turin: Giappichelli, 2021.

Garlati, L. & G.E. Vigevani (eds). *Processo e informazione.* Milano: Giuffré 2012.

Grandinetti, O. 'Il Testo unico dei servizi di media audiovisivi e radiofonici'. *Giornale di diritto amministrativo* (2011): 121 et seq.

Grandinetti, O. 'Par condicio e programmi di informazione'. *Giornale di diritto amministrativo* (2008): 1157 et seq.

Grandinetti, O. 'Il riparto di attribuzioni tra Autorità per le garanzie nelle comunicazioni e Ministero nella gestione delle radiofrequenze'. *Costituzionalismo.it* (2004): 6 et seq.

Luciani, M. 'La libertà di informazione nella giurisprudenza costituzionale italiana', *Politica del diritto* (1989): 605 et seq.

Mastroianni, R. & A. Arena. 'Rules on Market Access, Media Concentration, Competition Law, and Other Approaches to Limiting Market Power: Italy'. In *Converged Markets – Converged Power? Regulation and Case Law – IRIS Special,* edited by S. Nikoltchev. European Audiovisual Observatory, 2012, 111–121.

Mastroianni R., 'Country of origin e principio di territorialità', Media Laws, 1(2019).

Mastroianni, R. 'Il Protocollo sul sistema di radiodiffusione pubblica'. *Il Diritto dell'Unione Europea* (1998): 533 et seq.

Mastroianni, R. *La direttiva sui servizi di media audiovisivi e la sua attuazione nell'ordinamento italiano.* II ed., Turin: Giappichelli, 2011.

Mastroianni, R. 'Promoting Information Pluralism Through EU Law: Regulation or Competition Law in the Audiovisual Sector?'. In *EU Competition Law: Between Public and Private Enforcement,* edited by B. Cortese. Alphen aan den Rijn: Kluwer Law International, 2014, 333 et seq.

Mastroianni, R. *Riforma del sistema radiotelevisivo italiano e diritto europeo.* Turin: Giappichelli, 2004.

Mastroianni, R. 'Territorialità e Paese d'origine nelle direttive sui servizi di media audiovisivi e sulle pratiche commerciali sleali'. AIDA (2008): 3 et seq.

Mastroianni, R. 'Freedom and pluralism of the media: a European value waiting to be discovered?' MediaLaws, 3 (2021).

Pace, A. & M. Manetti. 'Art. 21: la libertà di manifestazione del proprio pensiero'. In *Commentario della Costituzione*, edited by G. Branca & A. Pizzorusso. Bologna: Zanichelli, 2006.

Pallotta, O. 'Servizio pubblico radiotelevisivo e integrazione culturale nel diritto UE e nel processo d'integrazione euromediterranea'. In *L'Europa e il Mediterraneo. Profili giuridici ed economici,* edited by S. Campailla, F. Mosconi. Bologna, Il Mulino, 2013, 89 et seq.

Papa, A., Il diritto dell'informazione e della comunicazione nell'era digitale, Giappichelli, 2021.

Pisillo Mazzeschi, R. et al. *Il diritto al pluralismo dell'informazione in Europa e in Italia*, Rai Eri: Roma, 2012.

Schepisi, C. 'Televisioni e aiuti di Stato: il finanziamento del servizio radiotelevisivo pubblico e gli aiuti per il passaggio al digitale terrestre'. AIDA (2010): 48 et seq.

Strozzi, G. 'La libertà dell'informazione nel diritto internazionale'. In *Nuove dimensioni dei diritti di libertà: scritti in onore di Paolo Barile.* Padua: Cedam, 1990, 669 et seq.

Vigevani, G. E., Pollicino, O., Melzi D'Eril C., Cuniberti M., Bassini M., Diritto dell'informazione e dei media, Giappichelli, 2022.

R. Zaccaria, A. Valastro, E. Albanesi, *Diritto dell'informazione e della comunicazione*, Padua: Cedam, 2021.

Index

The numbers here refer to paragraph numbers.

Index

www.ingramcontent.com/pod-product-compliance
Lightning Source LLC
Chambersburg PA
CBHW071351230926
51846CB00002B/507
9789403509471